POOR LAW

★ The mass arrest of homeless claimants in Oxford

by ROS FRANEY

Illustrated by Jim Stanes and Nina Carroll

● CHAR, Campaign for Single Homeless People
● Child Poverty Action Group
● Claimants' Defence Committee
● National Association of Probation Officers
● National Council for Civil Liberties

Poor Law
Published 1983 by
CHAR, Campaign for Single Homeless People
Child Poverty Action Group
Claimants' Defence Committee
National Association of Probation Officers
National Council for Civil Liberties

Design/Production: Roger Huddle (Artworkers)
Cover picture: Ken Thompson
Typeset/Printing: Lithosphere, London N1

ISBN 0 906951 04 6

Contents

Acknowledgements

Many thanks to Paul Bristow, Ian Bush, Walter Byrne, Anthony Kelleher, John Meiklejohn and all other arrested claimants whose statements appear in this report, but who wanted to remain anonymous. We would also like to thank the many people who provided evidence, advice and extensive background information.

The organisations who produced POOR LAW gratefully acknowledge the support of the Rowntree Social Services Trust.

Foreword

As one of the innocent people held for several hours during Operation Major, I should like to express my utter disgust at what happened to myself and the other unfortunate claimants on September 2, 1982. We were treated more like a herd of animals on the way to the slaughter house than human beings who'd come to pick up the measly allowance the Government makes us try and live on. We were held in appalling conditions, during which time all our rights were ignored. The police only acknowledged our existence when they felt the need to assert their authority over us. Young, old, sick and healthy – we were all treated as though we had just assassinated Norman Fowler. No thought was given to inform loved ones, friends or relatives of where we were, what had happened to us or when we might be released – if at all.

It's made me – and I dare say many others – realize that if you're out of work or drawing benefit you aren't classed as a human being any longer. You are just a government statistic which can be spied on, attacked, arrested, persecuted and used whenever and for whatever reason the bureaucrats and the capitalists think up.

I feel nothing but contempt and hatred towards the various people who took part in this sorrowful and costly operation, which attacks the poorest and most underprivileged section of society – including mentally handicapped, alcoholic, homeless and needy people. Such an operation should never have been thought about, let alone carried out.

I think it is really important for people from all walks of life to read this report and try to understand what it feels like to be homeless, unemployed and drawing benefit, and also to understand the difficulties we have faced during and since Operation Major.

Anthony Kelleher

Ken Thompson

Arrested man on his way to court, Sepember 2.

Introduction

On September 2 1982, 283 people who walked into an unemployment benefit office in Oxford found themselves arrested by the police on suspicion of fraud. The 'temporary' office where they had gone to sign on was a fake, set up by Thames Valley Police and the local Department of Health and Social Security (DHSS) to catch people who had been giving false addresses in order to claim extra money. They were held throughout the day in boarded-up rooms, and were denied the limited rights allowed to people under arrest.

A large number of those arrested were innocent. Some were not even claimants, but were merely accompanying friends. Over 100 people were held for up to 10 hours before being released without charge.

The rest appeared that afternoon and evening before special courts – whose proceedings were conducted quite differently from normal magistrates' court procedure. The accused were denied access to solicitors before appearing in front of the magistrates, so most of them had no legal representation and only a handful managed to get bail. The great majority were held in custody until a later date.

Relatives, city councillors, probation officers and social workers were kept in the dark about who had been arrested and what would happen to them. Yet the police had been careful to arrange for prior information to be given to the media. Press and television reported the story in detail as a crime drama which seriously exaggerated the extent of the fraud.

The police called it "Operation Major" and were prompt to suggest links with organised crime. Yet the landlords at the centre of the affair escaped scot-free and, although picked up briefly for questioning, were allowed to continue their livelihood unimpeded by police investigations. The landlords became principal witnesses for the prosecution, but their evidence in court was too unreliable to be of use. A statement by one of them which was used to convict some of the claimants proved to be of dubious legitimacy.

The Oxford Unemployed Workers' and Claimants' Union* responded swiftly to Operation Major. It mounted a demonstration on the afternoon of the arrests and took statements from those who had been arrested and released. Two days later, on September 4, it called a public meeting which was attended by a large number of solicitors, claimants, city and county councillors, trades union representatives, probation officers, welfare and civil rights workers and many others who were horrified by what had happened. The Claimants' Defence Committee was set up at this meeting with the aim of monitoring the court hearings and publicising the issues raised by the operation.

Perhaps the only good to come out of Operation Major is the way in which it has alerted people to the difficulties faced by the unemployed and homeless and the concern it has raised across the political spectrum. The operation has been condemned by the Labour Party Conference and by Labour and Conservative politicians as well as by the civil service unions, the National Association of Probation Officers, the Oxford Trades Council and many voluntary agencies.

The strength of this concern brought together our five organisations to produce a joint report. This report examines the facts of the Oxford arrests, the problems which gave rise to them and the issues they generate. Its primary sources are the statements of those arrested and the people attempting to defend them, while the recommendations which conclude it represent the policies relevant to each organisation and are not all necessarily endorsed by the full group.

The aim of the report is to redress the balance of a sophisticated and successful public relations exercise mounted by the police and

* Referred to as the Claimants' Union throughout this report.

the DHSS against claimants, which was reported largely without challenge by the media. It charts the experience of those arrested and investigates breaches of civil liberties and procedures by the police and the courts. It questions the adequacy of the supplementary benefit system and the part played by the local DHSS, which saw the operation as a means of solving its severe staffing problems in the face of a rapidly increasing caseload. It scrutinises the role of the private landlords and the way they thrive on the back of an ailing and inadequate system of benefits and housing provision. Finally, and more broadly, it looks at the housing crisis facing single people and the reasons why it affects Oxford so severely. Without the housing crisis there would have been no fraud in the first place: the claimants who defrauded the DHSS because they were homeless would have been entitled to that extra benefit if they had had a place to live.

1 THE POLICE

The plan

Chief Constable Peter Imbert told a meeting of the Thames Valley Police Authority on September 24 1982 that the police became involved in the matter of DHSS fraud in Oxford coincidentally in April 1982, during the course of another "major enquiry". This was in fact a murder investigation in the city. Addresses found on a suspect led the police to make enquiries into boarding houses used by single homeless people. The numbers of claimants to have registered these addresses with the DHSS significantly exceeded the capacity of the boarding houses. This aroused police suspicions that the places were being used as accommodation addresses by homeless people in order to claim benefit at a higher rate than they would otherwise be entitled to.

But the police were not the only ones to be investigating the matter. Peter McIntyre, social services reporter with the *Oxford Mail* who was writing a series of articles on the city's acute housing problems, followed up allegations that landlords were overcrowding their boarding houses and taking money from homeless people who were not actually living there.

In the second week of July, McIntyre interviewed Meurig Jones, manager of the local DHSS office. He asked how much Jones' department spent on funding claimants in bed and breakfast; how much of this money went to individual landlords; and whether the DHSS kept checks on the conditions in which claimants were living. The manager was unable to answer these questions because, he said, a police investigation was in progress into the matter. A couple of days later McIntyre's editor received a visit from the police who told him to drop the story because the *Mail*'s investigations were pre-empting their own. McIntyre was summoned to an interview with Detective Inspector Roy Payne at St Aldates police station. At this brief interview, McIntyre asked who the police were moving against and Payne said "the landlords". McIntyre took this to mean that there would be some kind of raid on the boarding houses in which books would be seized and the landlords arrested.

But it was against the claimants, not the landlords, that police were mounting an elaborate operation. They called it "Operation Major" and planned it in consultation with the DHSS. Operation Major was top secret. The only people who allegedly knew of it in advance were George Currill, chairman of the Oxford magistrates; Jim Biggin, the Clerk to the Justices; senior officers of the local DHSS – and, at the last minute, the press.

The *Oxford Mail* reported that few local police knew what was going on until the last moment. The operation was handled by the Bicester-based Serious Crimes Squad headed by Detective Superintendent George Hedges, with Detective Inspector Roy Payne in charge of operations. "They worked from a small flat on the third floor of St Aldates police station with their own ex-directory telephone working independently of the station switchboard and with their own back stairway entrance", reported the *Mail* on September 2.

For the purposes of the operation, the DHSS hired a disused school from Oxfordshire County Council. The South Oxford Middle School, which had been leased to them before to take an overspill from the regular social security office, was handed over via the Property Services Agency by Peter Audley-Miller, Conservative chairman of the Land, Buildings and Supplies Committee. The powers he used did not require him to consult his committee members. The DHSS paid a rent of £2,200 between August 4 and September 24 (*Hansard*, November 8, col 79).

The DHSS then sent out the following notice to selected claimants:

SPECIAL NOTICE

IN ORDER TO EASE OVERCROWDING OF UNEMPLOYMENT BENEFIT OFFICES A TEMPORARY BENEFIT OFFICE HAS BEEN OPENED AT SOUTH OXFORD MIDDLE SCHOOL, CROMWELL STREET (SEE MAP BELOW) FOR THE ISSUE OF GIROCHEQUES TO PERSONAL ISSUE CLAIMANTS.

FROM NEXT WEEK, THURSDAY 26TH AUGUST, YOU SHOULD ATTEND AT THAT ADDRESS AT THE *NEW SIGNING TIME SHOWN ON THE ATTACHED CARD (UB 40).* PLEASE ENSURE THAT YOU ATTEND AT THE TIME STATED. THE TEMPORARY OFFICE WILL BE *OPEN ON THURSDAYS ONLY.* ENQUIRIES ON OTHER DAYS WILL BE DEALT WITH AT YOUR NORMAL OFFICE.

The claimants duly signed on at the South Oxford Middle School on August 26 and collected their giros as usual. Everything seemed normal.

Over the following week, the final touches were put to Operation Major: the police arranged for men to be at work on a site next to the school – making noise to drown any shouts of warning from those arrested to those outside; they set up video cameras in the school to film the whole operation; they held a 'rehearsal' with senior DHSS officers to arrange the procedure for the arrests; and permission was obtained from the Home Office to move 80 people out of Oxford Prison on September 1, leaving a wing clear for those arrested (in the event it wasn't enough). Finally, the police alerted the media.

On the afternoon of September 1, the day before the operation, Geoff Meade of Central Television was contacted by the police:

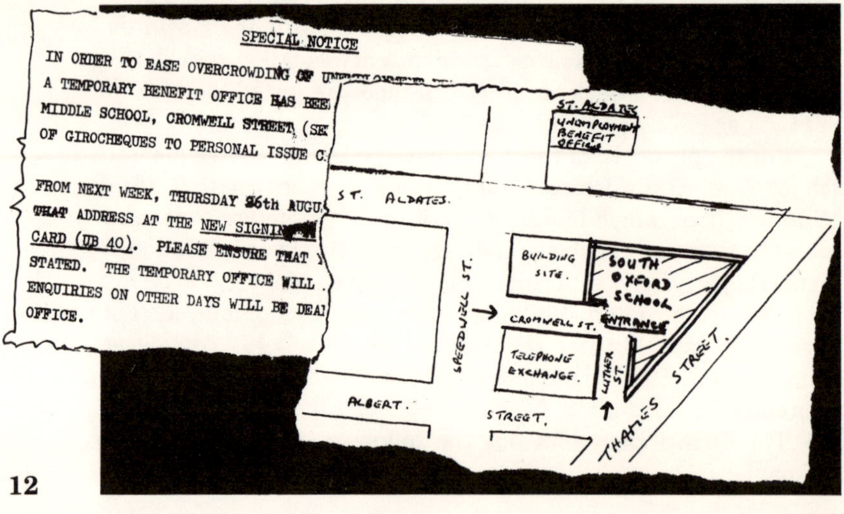

"They said there was going to be a major operation involving large numbers of arrests and that South Oxford Middle School would be used to detain prisoners. We wanted to get a film crew to the scene but the police didn't want us outside too early because they said it would frighten off the people who were to be arrested. They said this was the culmination of months of planning and asked us to respect the need for secrecy. We looked for a building nearby where we could film without being seen, but there was nothing suitable. The next morning I went to St Aldates police station where a press office had been set up, and that was the first I knew that the arrests were going to be of people involved in benefit fraud."

While the Police Authority was being told that press were not notified until midday of September 2, Assistant Chief Constable Jones was simultaneously admitting to a member of the BBC *Grapevine* team that the press had been alerted 24 hours earlier. The *Oxford Mail* detailed several reporters in advance to leave Thursday afternoon free so that they could cover the special courts. Radio Oxford was also tipped off a day in advance.

Dawn raid

Between six and seven in the morning on September 2, police raided the boarding houses of an Oxford landlord, Jeremiah Cronin. No one saw the warrant for this, though it was alleged to be a warrant under the Prevention of Terrorism Act. The police went into each room and took details of people living there. No one was

South Oxford Middle School.

arrested. According to one resident of 137 Iffley Road (one of the addresses), "I was woken at 7 am by a plainclothes police officer who wanted to see who was there and if I was in London at the time of the bombs". With another man, Anthony Kelleher, the following exchange took place:

"Have you been in London?"

"When?"

"Between the 18th and the 21st July, when the bandstand got blown up."

"Is that what you're here for?"

"Yes."

A third man who was asked the same question, said the police took his name, height, date and place of birth. But a man who told them he *had* been in London at the time of the bombs said the police didn't seem interested.

It appears that the purpose of the raid was to establish who were the actual residents. But the police used this information selectively: those who *were* sleeping at Cronin's were held for several hours on arrest although the police knew them to be innocent. One man – Walter Byrne – who was sleeping there but who had gone out very early, was charged on the 'evidence' of the police raid (ie that he *hadn't* been there). When his case was eventually heard the court found there was no case to answer. By that time he had spent 21 days in prison.

The operation

Inside

At 9 am on September 2, the claimants began to arrive at the South Oxford Middle School to sign on for the second week. One of the first was 16-year-old Ian Bush: "They told me to go through a door behind me. I said, 'I'll go out the other door I came in 'cos I know where I've been', but two supposed workmen with an electric drill who were watching me through the door, said, 'this way's quicker'. I knew something was up because they were drilling the carpet. I stepped two feet through the door. The door sprang back and two policemen grabbed me and said, 'you're under arrest for trying to obtain money by deception from the DHSS'.

"They walked me into a corridor where I was guarded along with 10 other people by about 40 to 50 police. I started to ask what was going on. I thought it was a bit of a joke. They said, 'you'll find out if it's a joke or not when you get in there'. I was led into a big hall.

I thought it was a police convention when I got inside. I was stood at a desk, had my name and a number written down on a piece of paper. I was then led to another area where I had my photograph taken with a Polaroid camera, holding the paper with my name and number in front of me. I said, 'what's happening?' and a policeman holding me by the arm said, 'you're famous'. People on the desks – about 30 desks – were all dressed in police uniforms. Photographers – I saw two – were wearing ordinary clothes. I was pushed through people by the policeman from behind, all the way down through the hall. I was forced to bump into loads of people and a desk.

"At the desk I was told to take all my jewellery off, shoelaces out and empty my pockets. In fact he insisted on going through my pockets and found a penny. Then he said, 'what about the watch?' I replied, 'It stays on my wrist'. He said, 'either you take it off or you go into a room with a lot of policemen and we'll take it off you'. I thought that meant they'd beat me up, so I wasn't left with a choice about taking it off. I couldn't see why they wanted it."

A few of those arrested were informed of their rights, but many were not: "We were not told what our rights were by any police officers and there were no visible notices on the walls"; "We didn't get to read what we were entitled to until after it was all over because of the confusion." The statements are unanimous in that the only room which had a notice on the wall informing prisoners of their rights was the one in which they were put at the end, while waiting to be released. "I asked to phone my solicitor and my girlfriend", said a man. "The policeman said no as it would hinder their investigations." "I asked to see my solicitor," said another man, "and they told me I must be joking". No one was allowed to make the phone call to which they should have been entitled, and not one of the 175 people charged saw a solicitor before going to the courts.

As they were arrested, the claimants were put in rooms – 60 or more to a room – which had the windows boarded up and no ventilation. It was a very hot day. At lunchtime the police distributed sandwiches, crisps, biscuits, an apple and a cup of tea to each person. "I was in room 5", said Anthony Kelleher. "It had chairs running round the walls and ending at a desk on the other side of the door which was manned by four or five police officers. There was also another row of chairs in a square in the middle of the room. There were about 80 chairs altogether, which were quickly occupied over about an hour. We had no facilities for obtaining water and hardly any ventilation. In fact the only air we received was through the open door leading to the main hall. We were not allowed to stand up or walk around during the whole time we were in there."

Indiscriminate arrests

Some of those who walked into the school hadn't come to sign on but were merely accompanying friends. A young woman went in with her friend and was arrested, despite the fact that she was not a claimant. She repeatedly told the police that she must leave to go and pick up her baby, but was nonetheless held for nearly four hours before being released without charge. One man who went to sign on had only moved to one of the suspect addresses (59 Western Road) two days previously. He was arrested, together with his wife who is epileptic. He pleaded with the police at least to release his wife, but was told not to interfere. Her property, except for two of her pills for epilepsy and an inhaler, was confiscated. During the course of the afternoon her period started and she had to wait half an hour for a policewoman to provide her with two pieces of toilet paper – the only protection on hand. Husband and wife were 'processed' separately: he was released at 3.40 but she was held until 4.30.

A youth who was not one of the claimants accompanied his friend to sign on and was held for 10½ hours. At one point he was strip-searched in public because police suspected him of carrying drugs. Along with many others he was held for two further hours even after they had told him he would not be charged. It was 8 pm before he was allowed to leave the building.

Sylvia went to the school at midday to look for the man she lived with. He'd gone for the rent money and hadn't come back. "As soon as I got inside, I could see he wasn't there, so I turned to leave and this bloke said, 'you can go out this way if you like'. I went the way he said, and suddenly I was surrounded by policemen. They asked me where my giro was. I said I hadn't got one, I'd come looking for my friend. It made no difference. I was still arrested and photographed. 'Hold on to this number,' they told me. 'I'm not holding no number,' I said. '*You* flippin hold it!' They took my handbag away. The room was full of blokes, but it was dead quiet. When I wanted to go to the toilet, a policewoman came along and held on to me. The place was crawling with policemen. They were grabbing hold of blokes by their shirts. There were police dogs in the yard." According to another man, "There were bleeding great alsatians sitting outside the toilets, but the dogs were with handlers".

One young man refused to be photographed and was kept overnight in a police cell. "They kept saying you're not going till we've got your photo. I told them I didn't care, I can wait if they can. I wouldn't let them take nothing off me in the school. I was taken over to St Aldates and put in a cell. The police station was packed. After a couple of hours a policeman came in and said, 'Look, let us have your photo and we'll give you bail'. So I said, 'I've been charged with nothing, so let me out of here'. He said, 'stop messing about, just give us your photo and behave yourself and you'll get out'. I told him to go away (not so politely). He came back about 10.30 and said, 'have you decided to give us your photo yet?' I remember saying, 'if you want a photograph get a court order for it'. they just left me all night then. I got nothing from 3.00 onwards, till the morning – no tea, coffee, nothing. No water." He was released next morning without charge.

Slowly, throughout the afternoon, those who were not charged were released. Many of them were held for six to eight hours. A mentally handicapped youth, who had been living at Cronin's for over a year, was held for seven hours and not allowed to see anyone although he repeatedly asked for his social worker to be notified. This allegation was investigated and confirmed by the County Council social services committee although the police denied all knowledge of it at the Police Authority meeting on September 24. One man lost a place to live because of being arrested: "I was supposed to report for it at midday. The person held the flat till 4 o'clock but it was 6.15 when I got out, so I was made homeless."

At their September 2 press conference the police claimed they had a doctor on call. Yet a man suffering from DTs was left without medical help. They put the man on the floor in a corner between two chairs. When asked was he all right, Anthony Kelleher, who was in the same room, replied that he was, at which the officer commented, "I'm not really concerned about him. He can have a wank for all I care."

By the evening conditions were becoming unbearable: "At about 7 pm we were removed into another room, already full of people", said a man held for over 10 hours before being released without charge. "This room now contained approximately 120 people. There was standing room only. We could not breathe." But eventually those not charged were released. "As I was released, a policeman said: 'you were arrested today on suspicion of obtaining money by deception. We are not charging you because of insufficient evidence'. This was the worst of all, that they did not clear you and say that you were innocent. I said, 'What d'you mean, "because of insufficient evidence"?' He said: 'that's their business'." When they were released, some, but not all, were given their giros back. Many were released too late to cash their giros at the post office and had to sleep rough on Thursday night.

The Claimants' Union received a statement from one man that he was fingerprinted without being charged: "I was fingerprinted. I was not asked if I was willing to have my fingerprints taken. When they released me they would not give my photograph or fingerprints back." Another man stated: "They told me there was no charge but they insisted that I let them take my fingerprints before I could go". "I said, 'can I have my photograph, please?' " said a third man. "He said, 'no, we're keeping it for the records'. I said, 'I'm innocent, that's why I'm being released. That's why I want my photograph back.' He said with a smirk on his face, 'that's not my fault. You're not getting it.' I was then taken out to the back yard and there was two police vans, a plain car and two or three coppers with dogs. A young copper said, 'don't come back, mate, otherwise the dogs will have you'."

Jim Stanes

Outside

By mid-morning a knot of people had gathered at the school gates, puzzled at why no one was coming out. One or two, like Sylvia, went in to look for their friends and got arrested. The

Claimants' Union were unaware of anything unusual until Peter McIntyre went to their office at 11 o'clock to warn them that "something" was up (though he didn't know what). News of the arrests actually reached them about 12.45 when Geoff Meade of Central Television rang up to ask them for an interview – it was disturbing that the press were the only body with any information to give. From 4 o'clock the Claimants' Union mounted a demonstration outside the South Oxford Middle School.

The police plans had included the establishment of a press office to brief journalists, but had omitted any provision for briefing solicitors, probation officers or social workers. Even the police on duty at the special courts had no information. That its organisers wanted to keep the operation secret from the public for as long as possible was crudely demonstrated by the police policy of arresting anyone who went into the school to enquire. Later, at the Thames Valley Police Authority meeting on September 24, this was confirmed by one of the members, Mr N.S.F. Douglass, who observed that it had been important to keep the innocent under arrest as well as the guilty, because otherwise they would have "warned the villains". Detective Superintendent Hedges told the press at the September 2 press conference that "we knocked off everyone who went into the building". He added that he had no doubt that some of those arrested were innocent.

A strict press embargo of 1pm had been agreed with those journalists who knew in advance. Most of the rest of the national press were tipped off mid-morning by the police press office, chiefly by phone calls to reporters in the area, and invited to a press conference at 2pm that day. The majority of national newspapers were represented at the press conference. The rest picked up the story from the media and sent their own people later on. About 12 general reporters attended at 2 o'clock: according to a local journalist, there were four from Fleet Street; two freelances; the local press and several 'area' reporters. A short statement by Detective Superintendent Hedges was followed by 30 minutes' questions and answers.

The briefing was thorough. A DHSS information officer gave details of the benefit rates and other technical information, and the DHSS was thus equally responsible, with the police, for the myths which were subsequently perpetrated by the media. One of the most serious of these was that a saving of £1½ million in benefit fraud had been achieved by the operation. This figure, which was reported throughout the national media, was later proved to be a serious over-estimate.

To relatives, friends and city councillors, the police were less forthcoming. They claimed at the Police Authority meeting that the press office received no calls about individuals, but this is likely to be attributable to public confusion over what was happening, and to the fact that most people didn't know who to turn to for information. Such information was not, in any case, easy to acquire, as illustrated by the experience of Labour Councillor Peter Moss, in whose ward Cronin's lodging house is situated:–

"I arrived home at about 6 pm and found a number of messages from people who were very worried and trying to find out about their friends and relatives who might have been arrested. I immediately went to St Aldates and asked the officer on duty. He said he was unable to help me because 'it was all being handled from upstairs' and he had been given no information. I insisted that I was keen to find someone who would be able to answer my questions because so many people were anxious, but I was told that the police were so busy and the operation had been so large that the only person who would be able to help me was the press officer. It wasn't possible to talk to her there, but I was given a separate phone number for her. I went home and telephoned, but of course by this time it was the evening and I was told I would have to wait until tomorrow. There was apparently no one at the police station who had a list of people under arrest; no one who could help the public outside office hours; and in any case there appeared to be a wall of secrecy between the normal police on duty and those handling this particular operation."

Those to be charged were taken in fives from the school to the courts handcuffed in police vans. People gathered outside the courts to try to find out who had been held. But the courts were no wiser than the police at St Aldates. The police officer in court whose job it was to liaise with the public had no information; there were no lists of the people who would be appearing; and defendants' names were either not announced over the tannoy or announced very indistinctly, so those potential sureties for bail who had managed to find out what was happening and get to the courts were not able to be on hand at the right time.

By the evening of September 2, 283 people had been arrested.* Of these, 104 were released without charge, 167 appeared before special courts and eight were given police bail to appear later.

* The Police changed their press conference statement of 286 to 283 on September 24. This figure conflicts with figures from the courts. See footnote on p27.

Almost all of those charged were remanded in custody: 74 people went to Oxford Prison, where they were joined the following day by 45 more. The rest were taken to Reading and Winchester jails and to High Wycombe Police Station. Only 15 got bail.

The police, the landlords and fabricated evidence

Jeremiah Cronin and Haribhai Patel, the two landlords of the suspect properties, were taken in for questioning by the police but released without charge. Mr Patel told ITN on September 3 that he kept records of everyone staying at his houses – an assertion which failed to stand up when he was cross-examined in court. Mr Cronin said: "my conscience is clear" (*Daily Telegraph*, September 11).

Cronin became the principal witness for the prosecution. He made a detailed statement to the police which was used as evidence against individual claimants (see Appendix 1). The statement was reproduced as a *pro forma*, at the bottom of which there was a blank space for the name of the defendant to be filled in afterwards. But Jeremiah Cronin had neither written nor signed the statement. It had in fact been drafted by the police, witnessed by a detective constable, and sent to Cronin for him to sign *afterwards.*

An unsigned copy of the *pro forma* evidence was obtained by the Claimants' Defence Committee and passed to Duncan Campbell of the *New Statesman.* Campbell telephoned the Thames Valley press office and told them he had the statement. "I said it appeared to me that the statement amounted to perjury. I did not make a formal complaint: I asked for a comment. I was 'phoned back by Deputy Chief Constable Leslie Emment, who treated my request for a comment as though I *had* made a complaint. He said he was asking for an outside police force [Gloucestershire] to investigate the accusation of fabricated evidence." The advantage of this for the police was that by initiating complaint proceedings they were

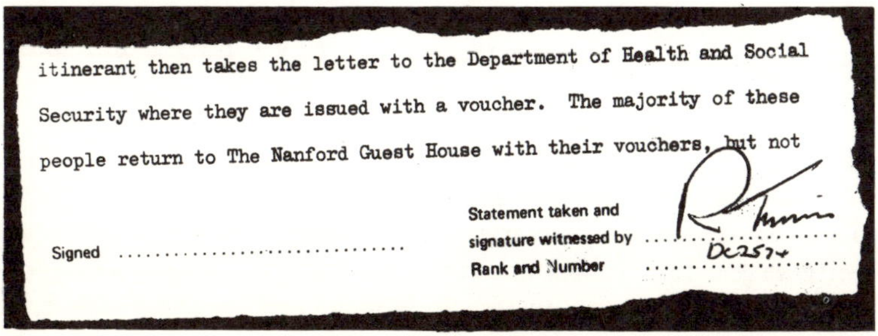
itinerant then takes the letter to the Department of Health and Social Security where they are issued with a voucher. The majority of these people return to The Nanford Guest House with their vouchers, but not

Signed ....

Statement taken and signature witnessed by ....

Rank and Number DC2574 ....

able to keep silent about Operation Major at the meetings of the Thames Valley Police Authority on September 24 and November 26 (see below).

In the event, though a report was sent to the Director of Public Prosecutions, the investigation didn't seem to amount to much. The detective constable who had countersigned Cronin's statement was still apparently attached to the fraud cases ("Campbell's in big trouble about that document", he is said to have remarked to Liz Fraser of the Claimants' Defence Committee outside the courts). The CDC was told by Chief Superintendent Dadge, who headed the investigation, that the statement would not have been used in court – it was "for information only". However the *pro forma* statement, signed by the same detective constable, was produced by the prosecution in other cases as the principal corroborating evidence.

The police answer questions

At the Thames Valley Police Authority meetings of September 24 and November 26, the police answered members' questions about Operation Major, although Chief Constable Peter Imbert said he was unable to make a detailed statement because of the pending investigation into alleged fabrication of evidence.

The answers to the questions were evasive and in some cases incomplete. Asked about delays in releasing the 104 people who were not charged, and about the detention of a mentally handicapped man for several hours, the chairman, Ron Clibbon, answered that he was not aware of either allegation and that the innocent were allowed to be released as soon as was "practicable". The police insisted that 25 notices of prisoners' rights were clearly displayed in the school where the claimants were held. Everyone signed the detention sheet saying they had been informed of their rights, the police claimed, and no one was fingerprinted who was not charged. Unfortunately, the police video of the operation, which showed all those arrested (including those not charged), could not be made available "in the interests of those who were held and later released".

The police also denied that difficulty had been experienced by people wanting to find out about those under arrest. A press office set up for the purpose received no enquiries, they said. With regard to bail arrangements, "everyone in custody was attended to as swiftly as possible". These answers did nothing to inspire confidence in the police authority system as a means of ensuring effective accountability.

Summary

A number of questions need to be posed concerning the police role in the operation:–

Why involve the police?

The DHSS has its own mechanism for dealing with benefit fraud, which is cheaper and less stigmatising than a full-scale police operation, as well as arguably more effective in putting a stop to fraud. The very involvement of the police in DHSS affairs is a cause for serious concern. Large scale tax frauds are prosecuted not by the police but by the Inland Revenue.

Why were human and civil rights suspended?

Police complacency about arresting everyone entering the South Oxford Middle School and holding them for several hours – even though many were known to have no connection with the fraud – must be condemned for its blatant disregard for human rights.

Despite police assertions to the contrary, those arrested insist that notices of their rights were not widely displayed at the bogus UBO. When phone calls and requests to solicitors were denied, no attempt was made to explain the reason (in contrast to Thames Valley Police's behaviour in front of the TV cameras in 'Operation Carter' (BBC, 1982) when they went to some lengths to explain prisoners' rights – or why they were being denied – to those under arrest). Detainees who were released without charge received no assurance that their particulars, photographs, fingerprints and the video film which had been taken while they were in custody would not be stored in police files and used against them in future. No explanation has been given by the police as to why – despite the weeks of planning – no arrangements were made for probation officers, solicitors, social workers and relatives to be informed about what had happened, while the press were given full details.

Why move against claimants and not landlords?

Police were eager to hint to the press that the fraud was organised on a grand scale. They spoke of "Mr Big". Yet they launched an operation against claimants which left "Mr Big" untouched – although, in their statement to Peter McIntyre and his editor, their original intention had been to move against a landlord or landlords.

Claimants treated as criminals

The harsh and punitive attitude towards claimants generally, and the equation of 'claimant' with 'criminal', was implicit in the arresting of every claimant who entered the fake benefit office. This, reinforced by information fed by the police and DHSS to the press both at the press conference and subsequently, made the whole operation look like a campaign against those on benefit.

The alleged 'savings' of £1.5 million are a serious over-estimate

For the Police/DHSS figure of £1½ million of fraud to be correct, each claimant charged would have had to be fiddling benefit continously for almost 3½ years. (It is important to take into account the fact that homeless claimants are entitled to the NFA (no fixed address) rate of benefit, so even those accused of wrongly claiming £67.20 are actually entitled to at least £18.60 of that sum.)

Therefore, *for the £1,500,000 to be correct:*

> The difference between the NFA rate and the full rate of £67 is **£49**, giving the number of claimant-weeks fiddled as **30,612**. Dividing this by the number of claimants charged (175) gives the number of weeks each claimant would have to have fiddled as **174.92**.

So each claimant would have to have made fraudulent claims for **3.4** years for the £1.5 million figure to be correct.

Estimated actual fraud

From an analysis of the majority of cases (158 which had been dealt with by October 15), the actual amount of the fraud – adding the amount of the charges and offences taken into consideration against each claimant – is **£58,564**. This does not take into account the benefit that claimants would have been entitled to legitimately.*

Costs of the police operation

Against this sum, the following costs must be considered:– (see table)

---

* Besides the weekly rate to which each claimant would have been entitled, some of them may have been owed additional money. For example, the Claimants' Union believes that John Perkins, who served 30 days for defrauding the DHSS of £146, is actually owed £1,000 by the Department because he spent two years underclaiming. Mr Perkins, an invalid, was convicted by Oxford magistrates of claiming both invalidity and sickness benefit in September 1982. On examining his case, the Claimants' Union found that he had not been told of allowances to which he was entitled and that the calculations of his existing benefit were incorrect. *The Guardian*, which carried the story on December 3, reported that a social security officer visited John Perkins in prison and apologised for the mistakes, promising a review of his benefit when he was released. At the time of going to press, he was unable to lodge an appeal to claim the money because of the local DHSS strike.

Costs of the Police operation

			Source
Police	£13,277	overtime, September 2	Police Authority, September 24
	991	travelling/transport, September 2	
	832	catering, September 2	
	9,000	normal duty costs, September 2	Oxon County Council, full meeting, November 1982.
DHSS	21,000		*Hansard*, October 22, col 236.
Prison	122,720	@ £177/wk	From cases sentenced by October 15, less ⅓ for remission. (Rate for 1981 quoted by *Report on the Work of the Prison Dept.*)
Detention centre	5,616	@ £156/wk	
Borstal	6,880	@ £215/wk (female borstal)	
Magistrates' expenses, Sept. 2	230	@ £19 each for loss of earnings for a sitting of over 4 hrs + £4 each subsistance for sitting 4-8 hrs.	Magistrates' Association rates.
Total	£180,546		

Far from saving money, Operation Major has actually cost the taxpayer **£180,546** – which does not include the cost of bringing 175 prosecutions.

ARREST

The police have no general right to stop people in the street, make them answer questions or take them to police stations without arresting them. People are often asked to go to a police station to 'help with enquiries', but they do not have to go unless they are arrested.

RIGHT TO SILENCE

In some cases, people must give their names and addresses (mainly motoring, drugs, firearms and weapons offences). In all other cases, they do not have to say anything to the police, and do not have to make a statement. If they do choose to make a statement, it is better that they write it out themselves, and do not sign it until they have seen a solicitor.

WHAT THE POLICE SHOULD DO

The police should:

- Inform someone 'reasonably named' by the detained person that s/he has been arrested (unless it will hinder their enquiries);
- Caution the arrested person, telling him or her that s/he does not have to say anything, but that anything s/he says may be taken down in writing and given in evidence as soon as they have reasonable grounds for suspecting that an offence has been committed;
- Issue another caution as someone is charged, or if further questions are asked on a subsequent occasion;
- Record both their questions and the arrested person's answers in full in writing, and present them to the person to sign as a true record. It is better that the accused does not sign anything, however, until s/he has been allowed to see a solicitor;
- Make reasonable arrangements for the person's comfort and refreshment.

SEEING A SOLICITOR

The police should let any detained person see a solicitor, although they need not do so if this will hinder the investigation. In practice, this usually means that they do not let a person see a solicitor until after they have finished questioning.

FINGERPRINTING

The police have no right to fingerprint a person without consent before s/he is charged. If s/he is charged, however, they can apply to a magistrate's court for an order allowing them to take fingerprints, even without consent being given.

PHOTOGRAPHING

The police have no powers to photograph anyone at the police station. If someone refuses, however, there is little s/he can do except complain, if they still take photographs without consent. If a person is remanded in prison before trial, the police can apply to a magistrate's court for an order to take photographs.

JUVENILES

Many of the rights above are extended in the case of children under 17.

POLICE AND CRIMINAL EVIDENCE BILL

Many of the rights listed above will be drastically curtailed by the Government's new Police Bill, which will probably become law during 1983.

THE COURTS 2

The emergency courts of September 2

Five special courts sat in Oxford on September 2, from 3pm until 11 pm, to deal with the people who had been arrested at the bogus benefit office. The 10 magistrates, who were alerted in advance that they would have to sit late, hardly included any women because it was felt that women would be "cooking dinner and looking after their families and would be too busy to come out in the evening". The 10 (two for each court) were apparently unaware of the nature of the police operation.

The defendants did not enter pleas to specific charges but were remanded on "offences of obtaining property by deception" to appear in court at a future date: 152 were remanded in custody for up to seven days and 15 were granted bail to appear two weeks later. A further eight had been granted bail by the police, bringing the total charged to 175*.

Although special courts of this nature have no separate legal

* There is a discrepancy between statistics issued by the police and the courts. The police say that 283 people were arrested, of whom 104 were released without charge, leaving the number to be charged at 179. We have used the courts' figure for the purposes of our calculations.

status, they share features which distinguish them from ordinary hearings in magistrates' courts. Because of the need to deal quickly with large numbers of defendants on September 2, normal procedures were set aside and cases were dealt with in the same haphazard and peremptory fashion as those in the courts set up to deal with the 'riots' in April and July 1981. This type of court has been the subject of persistent controversy.

The difference between the Oxford hearings and those which follow civil disturbances, however, is that Operation Major was planned for several months and the police and the courts had ample warning of the extra work it would create. The general feeling was of a process that was unnecessarily rushed, without due consideration of all the facts, and it is clear that some basic civil rights were suspended.

The Probation Service and local solicitors had no prior knowledge of the special courts, although the *Oxford Mail* had information about them and printed the story in its second edition which goes to press about 12.30 – well before the courts had begun to sit.

Jim Stanes

Interview facilities suspended

The normal procedures in Oxford Magistrates' Courts allow probation officers as well as solicitors to interview clients in the cells before they appear in court. As far as solicitors are concerned, the interview is a defendant's statutory right. However, the Oxford

Probation Service has an informal arrangement with the police that defendants are given the additional opportunity of being seen by probation officers. This arrangement, which generally works well, could not exist without the support of the police. On September 2, the arrangement was suspended. The Sergeant normally in charge was clearly not in command. The area of the cells was crowded with policemen – many unfamiliar to probation officers and solicitors – and no facilities had been provided either for probation officers or for solicitors to interview clients.

At 5pm, a solicitor and four probation officers managed to get a meeting with Chief Inspector Scott who was in charge of prosecutions, only to be told that access to the cells was out of the question because of the scale of the operation. It was clear that no consideration had been given to the matter of interviews or representation in the planning of the whole event. The Chief Inspector in charge stated that he saw no reason for probation officers to be involved, despite their role of supplying information to the courts to help defendants obtain bail.

Defendants not represented

Solicitors who complained of the lack of access to defendants were assured that people appearing before the magistrates would be told that solicitors were available. But it was clear in court that very few defendants knew of their legal right to representation and only a few asked for solicitors. Oxford National Council for Civil Liberties noted that when a defendant in Court 5 actually did ask, the clerk ignored his request. Another defendant was told that he would be able to see a solicitor before appearing in court a second time.

Probation officers and solicitors were present in court when the courts started sitting, but it was three hours before any solicitors were able to get to their feet to say anything. Peter Butler, secretary of the Oxford and District Solicitors' Association, described the experience to *LAG Bulletin*: "From 3 pm until 5.55 pm solicitors were in the courts, making notes and talking to probation officers, basically trying to reach defendants. It was a horrible atmosphere, we were sitting there unable to do anything while the court was shelling them through. Probation officers were standing up to offer bail hostel places and were ignored. We didn't manage to have a solicitor take instructions from any defendant until 5.55. What was so shocking was that normally we have a court careful to protect people's rights and these were suspended." Another solicitor told

LAG Bulletin that the clerks' attitude to solicitors was that "we were merely after the legal aid money".

Only in Court 1 did a woman clerk eventually break ranks with her colleagues and make a point of ensuring that defendants were asked if they wanted a solicitor. Some defendants in Court 5 were also represented. But the courts recorded that out of the total of 167 who appeared before the special courts, only 20 had legal representation.

Most hearings lasted about four minutes. The clerk read the charge, the prosecution applied for custody and the request was granted by the magistrates. If the procedure was lengthened at all it was only to read out a list of previous convictions or to hear rehearsals of evidence by the prosecution as to why a defendant should not be given bail. Throughout the evening the courts were made aware that probation officers were available, but they were rarely given the opportunity to speak – there was time to hear evidence when it was *against* bail, but not when it was in favour. There was no information on who was appearing, and probation officers were unable to prepare any information for the court which would have confirmed their clients' 'local' status or any available accommodation for the purposes of bail.

Bail withheld

Among the 152 defendants remanded in custody there were many who had never been in prison before, or even in a court. Many had addresses in Oxford where they could stay, as well as friends, relatives and probation officers to confirm the fact.

The Bail Act 1980 introduced the concept of "the presumption of the right to bail". Courts are directed only to refuse bail under specific circumstances and are instructed that they must state their reasons for doing so. On September 2, the reasons given were either the seriousness of the offence and the likelihood of further offences being committed if the defendant were to be given bail; or that the defendant had no community ties and the prosecution's fear that he or she would fail to surrender to custody.

With the first of these 'reasons', the police would normally be expected to give information on the gravity of the offence (usually involving violence or large sums of money) and also evidence of previous occasions when the defendant had committed offences while on bail. If, on the other hand, the court suggests that a defendant has no fixed address and is likely not to surrender to custody, a representing solicitor would normally help the defendant offer safe or reliable addresses, sureties from friends and a condition of daily reporting at a police station. On September 2, none of this was explored. Without the benefit of legal representation, the majority of defendants were unable to counter the police's request for a remand in custody and alternatives were not considered by the court. Furthermore, defendants were being prejudged as guilty: anyone who gave their address as 137 Iffley Road was being refused bail on the grounds that the address was suspect. Many defendants who gave other addresses had them rejected on the grounds, 'why should we believe you now when you have already lied once today about your address?' This happened notably in Court 4.

The Oxford Probation Service runs a 12-bed bail hostel in the city. At 3 o'clock, when the courts began to sit, it had four spare beds. Had the Probation Service been aware of an exceptional demand for emergency bail accommodation, this could have been arranged – as it actually was the following week when emergency bail hostel places were made available in Oxford and elsewhere.

But in order for consideration to be given for a bail hostel place, the defendant must be seen by a member of the Probation staff. The lack of access to defendants inhibited any of the necessary prerequisites and courts were unwilling to hold up a case even for a few minutes for possibilities to be discussed. When the special courts closed, there were still two empty beds for women in the local hostel, while one woman had been remanded in custody specifically because she had nowhere to go. When proper procedures were restored the following week, the courts granted bail to 32 of the 50 defendants whose cases were further adjourned.

The subsequent hearings

The sentencing policy of the courts

By Monday September 6, the courts were ready to start hearing the guilty pleas. Defendants were charged under section 15 of the Theft Act 1968 with obtaining property by deception. In Court 2 the hearings were actually delayed on the first day because the first case to be heard was evidently supposed to set the standard for the rest. The prosecuting solicitor was heard by Phil Cohen of *LAG Bulletin* to remark, "I'm told we can't go out of order because it will throw out the entire system". By the end of that week 152 people had been through the courts with the following results:–

Remands on bail	32	(at least half to bail hostels)
Detention Centre	3	
20 days in prison	4	
21-60	63	
61-100	18	
100+	12	
Suspended sentences	2	
Remands in custody	15	
Social enquiry reports	3	(all on bail)

The Claimants' Union demonstration outside the special courts.

Martin Stott

At a meeting of their General Purposes Committee, date unknown, Chairman of the magistrates George Currill and Deputy Chairman J.E. Critchley (attended by Jim Biggin, the Clerk to the Justices) agreed upon a sentencing tariff of 30 days' imprisonment for each giro of £67.20 fraudulently claimed, with some 15 days on top for extra offences to be taken into consideration. What seems to have happened is that most of the magistrates interpreted the tariff literally instead of using it merely for guidance. They were influenced by the emphasis which was placed on the seriousness of the offences and the sheer size of the operation. Many of the magistrates can be said to have panicked. They used the tariff to impose custodial sentences when in the normal course of events they should have remanded for social enquiry reports. Magistrates complained that defence solicitors had not prepared some of the cases properly and so were not producing enough information on their clients' backgrounds to warrant a more considered response. But in many cases probation officers were in court who had interviewed the defendants and did know a substantial amount: to them it appeared that the courts were to blame for being in too much of a hurry to bother with the details of each case.

Regardless of individual circumstances, the magistrates had abandoned the range of sentences available to them and were handing out much the same treatment to defendants with no previous convictions as to those with substantial records. This recourse to collective punishment, apart from imposing custodial sentences which were in many cases inappropriate, ignored one of the principles of British law: the concept of individualised justice. Phil Cohen of *LAG Bulletin*, who was in court, commented: "Solicitors attempted to make mitigation pleas on the basis of the individual circumstances of each case, though they did not (generally) affect the tariff. One prosecuting solicitor admitted to the bench, 'as you can understand, very little is known about these defendants'. Little real attempt was made to find out. Although in Court 2 the prosecution gave full details of the alleged offences, in Court 1 they did not – telling the bench in each case that they already knew the background from previous cases and therefore the charges would just be outlined." A prosecuting solicitor remarked to someone sitting behind the present writer in court: "It's rather like a limited-over cricket match. Things are a bit sluggish in the morning and the run-rate isn't very high, but once the eye is in the whole thing bowls along very nicely".

Together with the tariff came an agreement that under the circumstances it would be inappropriate to remand for social enquiry reports. Probation officers in court specifically requested social enquiry reports on 22 occasions, but only six were granted. In 'normal' circumstances, either when a client is known to the Service or when there are no previous convictions, probation officers say they would expect an adjournment for social enquiry reports – six out of 175 suggests emphatically that 'normal' processes were not operating. According to one of the clerks of the court responsible for collecting data about Operation Major, some 35%-40% of first offenders received custodial sentences.

This is completely out of proportion with practices recommended by the Home Office on sentencing in magistrates' courts and flies in the face of statements by the Judiciary. Both Lord Chief Justice Lane (head of the High Court) and Home Secretary William Whitelaw have counselled against the imposition of custodial sentences for both first and minor offences – as many of these were. The blanket effect of the tariff has been privately criticised by magistrates from other benches as an infringement of the individual magistrate's discretion to weigh up the circumstances of each case. Whether the Oxford magistrates are to blame for adhering too literally to the directive of their Chairman, or whether the nature of the directive made if difficult for them to take an individual stand, the end result must be an indictment of tariff sentencing.

Despite the tariff, there were anomalies. Interestingly, because of his implied acknowledgment that a tariff was operating, it was the Chief Clerk who brought defence solicitors' attention to section 142 of the Magistrates' Courts Act 1980. This section provides a 'slip rule' for the rectifying of mistakes in sentencing: it is not an appeal but allows for the same bench to be convened to reconsider a sentence, usually where there is thought to have been a miscarriage of justice. The circumstances of its use on this occasion were unusual in that the defence argued that the magistrates had not taken full account of the individual facts. Using section 142, sentences were successfully varied in three cases – one sentence was reduced from 90 to 60 days.

One solicitor noted that defendants whose cases were heard in the first few days seemed to be getting one or two charges against them and the rest 'taken into consideration' whereas, later on, more charges were being laid against defendants with correspondingly heavier sentences. This was particularly apparent among those pleading not guilty: one defendant actually had an extra charge added the second time he came up in court. He complained that had he pleaded guilty to begin with he would have got off more lightly. The court treated his complaint seriously and took it up with the prosecution, who said that no further charges would be added to the first two. In fact this particular defendant eventually had his case dismissed after 21 days in custody.

The landlords give evidence

In the third week of hearings, when the not guilty pleas began to come before the court, Cronin and Patel made their debut as witnesses for the prosecution. Jeremiah Cronin was the police's principal witness (he picked up expenses for his appearances – £18.85 on one occasion; £30 loss of earnings on another). But when he appeared in court, Cronin seemed unsure of the contents of the statement he was supposed to have made to the police, and indeed his evidence failed to stand up under cross-examination. He admitted that he did not keep a register and was unaware of who was staying at his four houses at any one time. "I would say you would be right to say I could not say definitely," he told the court. When asked how many people would be able to stay at once, it took him a very long time to answer. According to Adam Ganz of the Claimants' Union, who was in court, "he said, 'I'd like a few minutes to think about that', and started counting on his fingers". Eventually he said that 73 was the maximum with up to four people sharing a room. Following Cronin's evidence, most of the defendants pleading not guilty had their cases dismissed.

Haribhai Patel had strongly maintained – notably in an ITN interview on September 3 – that he kept records of everyone staying in his houses, but under cross-examination in the case of Timothy Sinclair (October 28) it emerged that his records were haphazard and contradictory. Information as to who was staying in his house was based mainly on telephone conversations with his son, Navnitchandru. The case was adjourned for Mr Patel Jr to be summoned to give evidence, but *he* said that records were made up partly from information given by a resident at 1 Iffley Road who acted as a caretaker. The hours he himself normally spent at the house (10 am - 3 pm) were the hours when residents were supposed to be out.

Police prosecutor John Wilcox asked for the case to be dropped. "It is quite apparent that the prosecution cannot prove Mr Sinclair was not staying there," he told the court. "It is only now it has become apparent that the records are hearsay". Magistrates

A claimant appears before the Oxford magistrates.

refused to let police costs be met from public funds and refused to pay Patel's expenses. Other defendants whose prosecution rested on the same evidence were subsequently acquitted. What was particularly reprehensible about the police's reliance on landlords' evidence – especially in the case of Patel – is that its fallibility was established at such a late stage. It seems clear that if more claimants had pleaded not guilty their pleas would have been upheld.

Guilty or not guilty?

Claimants were advised on their arrest that any absence from the address rendered them guilty. A claimant who was found guilty on a single charge had left the boarding house to go and visit his seriously ill mother in Wigan. The magistrates gave him a 'reduced' sentence of 21 days "in view of the mitigating circumstances".

It was not until the third week of hearings that under cross examination DHSS assistant manager John Minchell said that absence from the address for one night, or for the duration of a relative's illness, would not be regarded as a change of address. The claimant would only be expected to notify the DHSS of a permanent change. Several defendants were consequently acquitted on the grounds that their absence was temporary, because they were still to be regarded as resident at the address.

But in many earlier cases the argument had centred around whether the claimant was present or absent on a given night – not the same thing at all. For example, one claimant had maintained that he paid his rent but subsequently went to stay with his

---

SOCIAL ENQUIRY REPORTS

The Powers of Criminal Courts Act 1973 (PCCA) confers a general power on all criminal courts to ask for a probation officer's report to assist in determining the most suitable sentence (s46). A person who has never been in prison before may not be given a prison sentence unless the court is of the opinion that no other way of dealing with him/her is appropriate. To determine this, the court must consider both the circumstances and the relevant information about the accused (PCCA, ss19,20), and this should normally be obtained from a social enquiry report (Home Office Circular 233/1972, Explanatory Memorandum para 65). The Secretary of State has recommended that, as a normal practice, all courts should consider a social enquiry report before passing the following sentences on an offender aged 17 or over: detention in a detention centre; borstal training; imprisonment of a woman; imprisonment (including a suspended sentence) of up to two years when the offender has not received a previous prison sentence, including a suspended sentence (or borstal training).

daughter in Swindon. He pleaded not guilty but changed his plea against the advice of his solicitor because he had not obtained a receipt and would therefore (he insisted) not be able to prove his innocence; he wanted to "get it all over and done with", he said. He was given seven days' imprisonment.

His solicitor estimated that of the 30 or so clients she represented, about a third had pleaded guilty before their cases reached her when it appeared they should not have done. Another solicitor added that he had to cease acting for several clients "because you can't make a plea in mitigation for someone you believe to be innocent". The figures certainly show that defendants must have been under great pressure to plead guilty. In three cases claimants subsequently changed their pleas to not guilty. More might have done so but for the incentive to put the distressing experience behind them.

The not guilty pleas were still going through the courts at the time of going to press, but the majority had been dealt with by mid October (after that the turnover was very slow). The situation on October 15 was as follows:–

Total cases heard	158	
Cases still to be heard	17	(of which 7 pleading not guilty)
Of those 158 heard –		
Pleaded Not Guilty	19	
Pleaded Guilty	139	
Of the 139 Guilty pleas –		
Custodial sentences	137	
Suspended sentences	2	
Of the 19 Not Guilty pleas –		
Case dismissed	12	
Custodial sentences	4	
No case to answer	1	
Social enquiry reports	2	

The role of the Probation Service

During the first week of hearings, the courts were covered by a team of at least five probation officers with back-up provided by the whole of Oxfordshire Probation Service. The logistics of providing cover would have been less complicated to organise if the Probation Service had been given some prior warning of what was to come. Between them, two or three officers interviewed every defendant who wished to be seen (about 160 in the week). The purpose of this was to ensure that clients had access to solicitors: to assess them for bail hostels; to ascertain the need for social enquiry reports; and to respond to immediate social or domestic problems caused by their unexpected incarceration. Prison probation officers had also seen everyone remanded in custody and had forwarded relevant information.

The probation staff were able to arrange a network of bail and other suitable hostels distributed across the south of England. The Oxfordshire hostels (bail and probation) provided eight emergency beds on top of their normal resources. By the end of the week at least 18 hostels were providing beds on a daily basis.

Out of 44 requests for bail, 32 succeeded when the cases returned to court. This fact highlights the nature of the special courts on September 2, since there are no reasons why the people who were bailed subsequently should not have been given bail from the start.

The accused

The Claimants' Defence Committee (CDC) organised a rota of people to monitor every case as it came to court. A form was completed on each defendant which enabled the CDC to build up a profile of those who had been accused as well as information on the amount of each charge and the length of sentence. Their monitoring did not meet with the unqualified goodwill of the court staff: City Councillor Peter Moss reports that when he was covering one of the courts a clerk of the court said to him, "you're only here to make trouble".

The CDC's information confirmed the fact that those arrested and charged on September 2 were a disparate group of claimants. Some had previous convictions, others did not. The media made much of the notion that people were travelling from all over the country to claim in Oxford, but this is not borne out by an examination of defendants' origins. More than half (95) of the 175 in court were already known to the Oxford Probation Service, not necessarily because they were on probation, but because they were homeless and in the habit of using the Probation Day Centre (15 were on statutory orders at the time of Operation Major). But it is reasonable to conclude that most of those who were not already known to the Probation Service were nonetheless permanently living in Oxford. Many had no previous convictions and would therefore not be known anyway. Oxford has a large single homeless population, but when people come they tend to stay: only 20 of the total, when asked for an address in court on September 2, gave addresses outside the area. Probation officers know that many of the 20 were 'safe' addresses for bail – say, of relatives – whereas the defendant was in fact a long-term Oxford resident. Yet the incentive to give an address of some sort was very great, because it might enable the defendant to get bail. Thus the number who were actually resident outside the city must have been extremely small – probation officers knew of only two.

Prosecutions for benefit fraud – national trends

Theft Act or Supplementary Benefit Act

Prosecutions for benefit fraud may occur under the Theft Act 1968 or under the Supplementary Benefit (SB) Act 1976. Under the SB Act the maximum penalty is a fine of £1,000 or three months' imprisonment. Under the Theft Act the penalties can be heavier.* According to DHSS statistics, prosecution of frauds involving false addresses – the charge in the Oxford cases – is normally brought under the SB Act. To take the example of one nearby office – Cheltenham – 154 convictions were obtained in the year ending August 4 1981 (out of total contributory and supplementary benefit claims of 40,715), of which 27 were brought under the Theft Act. However, only two of these Theft Act prosecutions were for using a false address; the majority were for altered giros.

An exception to this rule appears to occur when the defrauding claimants are homeless. Statistics over the same period for two London offices (Thames North and Thames South) dealing primarily with claimants living in the capital's large lodging houses, show that out of a total 121,980 claims there were 145 prosecutions – all of them brought under the Theft Act. Of these, 34 were for using a false address (*Hansard*, November 18 1981, col 177).

From these figures it appears that 'homeless' claimants are dealt with in a more punitive way than others, and that the Oxford claimants were dealt with harshly even in comparison with other homeless people. Of the 33 prosecutions under the Theft Act in Thames North and Thames South for giving a false address in the year ending April 13 1982, 13 were given non-custodial sentences.

---

* A comparison may be drawn with the treatment of tax fraud, where the Inland Revenue may carry out its own investigations, independently of the police – even in cases where the amount of fraud is considerably greater than the entire sum involved in the Oxford benefit frauds (cf a case in Oxford of suspected tax fraud, p 54). The Inland Revenue can impose statutory financial penalties which, though they can be heavy, spare the offender the indignity either of prosecution or a prison sentence and leaves him or her with no criminal record.

This indication is reinforced by a written answer to Frank Field, MP for Birkenhead, in which Social Security Minister Hugh Rossi reported that "normally, proceedings [ie prosecution] would not be taken where overpayment was less than £50". Those convicted of a single offence in Oxford had actually defrauded the DHSS of £48.60 (*Hansard*, October 27 1982, col 445).

Double jeopardy

Claimants convicted of benefit fraud may be punished twice over. *LAG Bulletin* (October 1982, p119) has pointed out that according to the Duplication and Overpayment Regulations 1980 (Regulations 6 & 7), there may be a continuing liability to repay the debt defrauded via deduction from benefit of up to £4.90 a week. This deduction can – and has been – exacted even after a prison sentence has been served (though not, as yet, in any of the Oxford cases). Repayment is a factor of which magistrates ought to be aware before passing sentence, though it is unclear how the DHSS and the magistrates are supposed to guess at each others' intentions.

Summary

Points of concern arising out of the court hearings:–

Conduct of the special courts

1. Legal representation: In the great majority of cases, defendants were denied access to legal advice – their statutory right – before appearing in court.

2. Bail: Bail was denied to all but a few of those accused, contrary to the Bail Act 1980.

Individual justice ignored in the subsequent hearings

1. The tariff: The courts reacted to the mass arrests, as have other special courts before them, by handing out blanket sentences based on a crude tariff. Tariffs have limited uses – as in speeding offences, for example – but they are intended for guidance only. The tariff in these cases was too rigidly adhered to – partly because the magistrates had no choice, since they were under pressure to deal with the cases as fast as possible.

3. Social enquiry reports: Social enquiry reports were obtained in only six cases, with the result that, in the estimation of the clerks, "35% or 40%" of first offenders were given custodial sentences without alternatives being considered, contrary to recommendations from the Judiciary and as laid down in the Powers of Criminal Courts Act 1973 (explained in Home Office Circular 233/1972).

3. Confusion as to what constituted 'guilt': Several

defendants chose to plead guilty against the advice of their solicitors as the easier way out. But, independently of this, statements obtained from several claimants say the police told them they were guilty when they were in fact absent from the boarding house for a legitimate purpose. As a result, they pleaded guilty when they should not have done. This appears to be yet another consequence of the denial of legal advice at an early stage and the hurried way in which the cases were put through the courts in the first two weeks. It was only when the courts started hearing the not guilty pleas that evidence from landlords and DHSS officers resulted in the majority being acquitted. Had there been time for more thorough preparation, it is probable that a good many more defendants would have pleaded – and been found – not guilty.

AFTER ARREST

The police must grant bail unless they consider the offence to be serious or the arrested person is to be charged and brought before a magistrates' court within 24 hours of being arrested (48 hours at weekends). If they do not grant bail, then the arrested person should be allowed to contact a solicitor or friend to tell them the names and addresses of possible sureties.

AT THE MAGISTRATES' COURT

The accused person, or a lawyer acting on behalf of the accused, should ask the magistrates for bail. If s/he is accused of a minor offence, for which s/he cannot be sent to prison, s/he should be given bail unless s/he has previously failed to surrender to bail or has to be kept in custody for his or her own protection. Even if the alleged offence is more serious, s/he must still be given bail unless the court believes that s/he would fail to turn up for the trial, would interfere with witnesses, would commit another offence, or needs to be kept in custody for protection.

Various conditions can be imposed on bail, such as regular reporting to the police, surrendering of passports or not going to specified addresses.

Bail may be applied for after a remand for a medical or social enquiry report. It can be refused on any of the grounds mentioned above.

Any decisions by the magistrates about bail or conditions can be appealed against to a judge 'in chambers', i.e. sitting in private. A solicitor should be consulted about the procedure for this.

SURETIES

Sureties have to be prepared to swear under oath that they are willing to act for the accused person, and that they have sufficient funds. They have to be over 18 and have a permanent address.

IF THE MAGISTRATES REFUSE BAIL

If the case cannot be heard in one sitting, the accused can be remanded in custody for up to eight days. This will continue until the case is heard, or until s/he is committed for trial. If the accused is not legally represented at a first court appearance, s/he should apply for legal aid so that s/he can be represented on later appearances.

3 THE MEDIA

The media as public interrogator

A large part of the impetus behind Operation Major was its potential value as a public relations exercise. The Thames Valley Police have become well used to appearing on television over the past year (in Roger Graef's documentary series *The Police*, BBC 1982; *Operation Carter*, BBC 1982), and have clearly developed a sound sense of the power of the media which they exploited to their best advantage. To this end, they carefully stage-managed the part which would be played by press and television. They alerted TV crews in advance (see p.12) and held a press conference on the day itself at which all the details were put across *by the police themselves.*

The police were the source of virtually all the information released to the public. Their success was enhanced by the fact that at a 'slow' time of the year the coverage was huge, and with Parliament in recess there were no alternative authorities to qualify, contradict or even question what they were saying. The operation sparked no 'political row' which might have caused at least a partial backfire. On the contrary, the press exercise ran its course so smoothly that the police were able to issue follow-ups over the weekend which were perfect fodder for the media's scroungerphobia.

And because the police were the source of all news, significant questions were omitted – questions which most of the media apparently failed to ask. For example, there were few comparisons with tax fraud; no attention was paid to the large amounts of unclaimed benefit – estimated even by the DHSS to be £400 million a year; no question was posed about the nature and style of the operation and whether it was actually the most appropriate way of stopping the fraud; and few voices were raised at the denial of civil liberties to those arrested. Crucially, no one questioned the very presence of the police in a DHSS fraud investigation, or its implications for the concept of a welfare state.

The police concentrated on putting over a story which would be reported and dramatised as a crime in the context of a drama-documentary entertainment. The result was a celebration of police accomplishments.

The showbusiness image

The story that broke in the press on September 3 was a headline-writer's dream. Four of the tabloid newspapers likened the police operation to the Paul Newman/Robert Redford film *The Sting*, in which a fake betting office was set up to con a gambler out of his fortune. The analogy had undeniable appeal, though none of the papers chose to observe that those who set up the Sting in the film were villains themselves.

> THE STING: Police yesterday mounted a Sting-style operation to smash a massive social security racket. *(Daily Star)*
> THE STING: 286 netted in amazing dole swoop. *(The Sun)*
> THE AMAZING DOLE FIDDLE: a swindle that netted up to £1,500,000 in social security benefits was broken yesterday in a complex police operation rivaling the plot of the film 'The Sting'. *(Daily Mail)*
> THE STING: £1.5m fiddle smashed as 286 are held in bogus social security offices [*sic*] . . . all that was missing was the Scott Joplin piano music. *(Daily Express)*
> 286 ARE HELD IN DOLE FIDDLE and HOW THE DOLE CHEATS ARE TRAPPED *(Daily Mirror)*
> 286 HELD IN SWOOP ON BENEFITS RACKET *(Daily Telegraph)*
> POLICE SPRING BENEFIT TRAP ON 286 *(The Guardian)*
> 286 ARE HELD IN FRAUD RAID *(The Times)*
> DOWN-AND-OUTS ARRESTED IN POLICE SWOOP *(Morning Star)*

ITN made the same mistake as the *Mirror* and *The Sun* in the inaccurate use of "Dole" in its headline – ". . . that mass arrest of people claiming unemployment benefit" (*News at One*, September 3), thereby linking 'scroungers' to the unemployed. The mistake

DAILY STAR

FRIDAY, SEPTEMBER 3, 1982 15p Printed in London

DAILY STAR/MORI POLL EXCLUSIVE

Britain's trade unionists say: Give US the vote

By DAVID BUCHAN, Political Editor

BRITAIN'S trade unionists have overwhelmingly demanded the right to vote in secret before strikes are called.

This is a conclusion of a survey conducted exclusively for the Daily Star by Market and Opinion Research International during the run-up to next week's TUC Conference in Brighton.

People were asked whether strikes should be declared without first holding a secret ballot of all union members concerned. Among trade unionists alone, 84 per cent replied with a resounding NO.

Compelling

Union members felt even more strongly about the issue than did a general sample of people, who included non-unionists. In the general sample, 80 per cent were in favour of secret strike ballots.

The result will be a boost for Margaret Thatcher and her Cabinet, who want new laws compelling unions to hold private votes before launching industrial action.

But it will be a blow for many union leaders who remain opposed to balloting their members on key decisions.

As in many previous surveys, MORI found overwhelming agreement that unions have too much power. This view ...

Police set an amazing trap and arrest 286

POL

An arrested man is led away in handcuffs after questioning

THE STING

STAR REPORTER

POLICE yesterday mounted a Sting-style operation to smash a massive Social Security racket.

Detectives set up a fake DHSS office and arrested 286 people as they collected Giro cheques.

Just as in the film The Sting where a bogus ... was used as a trap police painstakingly ... office to crack a racket ...

OXFORD MAIL

No. 16,277 TUESDAY, SEPTEMBER 7, 1982 Price 12p

TV RENTAL SALES AND SERVICE Phone Oxford 48602 ILCO LTD

Curtains Plus

L-pupil had her bottom smacked

Get ready for spring: bulbs offer page 5

Police probe killer deal

THAMES VALLEY Police are to interview staff at Penguin Books following the news that the publishing giant made a deal with escaped Broadmoor killer Alan Reeve to publish his life story.

Search after dealer's murder

Solicitor tells of £50,000 fortunes

The greedy landlords

A LANDLORD ... made a fortune from the Oxford ... security fiddle, a solicitor alleged in court today.

Mr Peter Butler told Oxford magistrates ... £50,000 a year from ... hostel he ran over

Never too old for

was probably accidental, the subs' expedient use of language or ignorance of the difference between dole and benefit, but that doesn't excuse it. BBC TV *9 o'clock News* said: "Police smash an alleged million pound social security racket. 300 people arrested".

'Facts' and sources

The press agreed that "100" or "over 100" police were involved, except for the *Daily Mail* which put the number at "200". The actual figure, revealed by Chief Constable Imbert to the Police Authority meeting of November 26, was 213.

There was some confusion about how long the operation had taken to plan. *The Guardian* claimed "two months"; the *Express, Telegraph* and *Daily Star* doubled it ("16 weeks"), while the *Mail* said that the tip-off had come "four months ago" while the 'Sting' had taken a mere "two weeks" to prepare.

There was a rough consensus on the amount of public money saved by the operation, but with variety in the way the figure was presented: *The Sun* and the *Daily Star* reported simply a "one-and-a-half million pound social security racket" and a "£1.5m-a-year benefits swindle". The *Telegraph, Mail, Mirror* and BBC were slightly more cautious ("believed to total more than a million" (*Telegraph*); "up to £1.5m" (*Mail*). The *Express*, however, put the figure at "£1,500,000 – or more". So did *The Times* and ITN. *The Guardian* and the *Morning Star* wisely declined to give a figure at all.

Those papers to take the analogy from showbusiness proceeded to make the most of the drama. "Police put their own men alongside the real DHSS clerks," said the *Daily Star*. "Temporary counters were manned by detectives and Ministry Investigators, handcuffs as well as handouts at the ready," said the *Express*. The *Mail* described: "Plainclothes men, one as a punk complete with earring, kept watch in and outside", while *The Sun* spelt it out: "Policemen disguised as hippies and punks were posted outside to make the place look like the usual DHSS establishment".

The police were recognised as the source of all the information: "An officer said. . ."; "Police report. . ."; "According to the police prosecutor. . .'. The *Express* and ITN also drew on the information "a Ministry investigator" and "investigators from the DHSS". " 'They came in like lambs to the slaughter', said a policeman" (*Daily Express*).

Almost all the dailies had details of the police video cameras and the nearby workmen who had been laid on to "drown out the warning cries of those arrested". Similarly, almost all reported (usually in a sentence towards the end) the statement by Detective Superintendent George Hedges that some of those arrested were likely to be legitimate claimants and would be released. But the media did not question the legitimacy of arresting them in the first place.

Civil rights

There was universal respect for the efficiency of the operation. Even the comments of released claimants were marshalled in evidence of this – "it was like Belsen", quoted an admiring *Sun.* Although the *Telegraph, Sun* and *Express* all published brief quotes from people who had been arrested and released, none of them, remarkably, followed up these allegations to question whether human rights had been violated. On the contrary, the press were careful not to suggest that police behaviour might have been anything other than sporting. Claimants were "ushered" through a doorway "into the arms" of waiting policemen. According to the *Daily Star*: "We wanted to ensure everyone was treated in the very best style,' an officer said. 'We even arranged for the lavatory to be spick and span for them'." Most of the papers reported that "hot drinks and food were laid on and a doctor was on call".

Unfortunately, none of the reporters apparently thought to ask whether access to legal facilities had also been arranged. Only *The Guardian*, in a quote from the Claimants' Union on September 3 and from the Oxford and District Solicitors' association on September 4, suggested at an early stage that there might be another side to the story. Not one newspaper questioned the conduct of the police or the omission of civil rights from the carefully laid plans. One could excuse press ignorance of the details and context of the benefit system, but police and court procedure is far more widely understood among reporters, and the failure to raise points about the irregular way in which large numbers of people were arrested and tried in Operation Major is a disturbing omission. On September 5 BBC Radio 4's *The World This Weekend* did broadcast an interview with 16-year-old Paul Bristow, who had been arrested and released, in which Bristow said he had been held for eight hours without charge and had not been allowed to contact anyone. But apart from this, no national newspaper or TV programme – with the honourable exception, later on, of the BBC's *Grapevine* – published details of the way civil rights had been denied to those arrested.

The media's concern, or lack of it, for civil rights tends to fluctuate according to whose rights are being violated. In his book *Images of Welfare*, Peter Golding cites the outrage of Lord Denning, and behind him the press, when Inland Revenue officials raided the home of a banker under suspicion of tax fraud – "Tax Men Blasted" (*Daily Express* August 17, 1979); "Taming of the Tax Man" (*Daily Mail*). Lord Denning's photograph was captioned: "The Judge who fights for freedom". The media was not interested in fighting for freedom on behalf of the claimants in Oxford. The Claimants' Union, who tried, got a rap on the knuckles from the *Daily Express* (September 4) for "turning morality on its head".

A *Sunday Times* reporter was the only national newspaper journalist at a press conference given by the Claimants' Union on September 4, and a short news piece appeared the next day ("Benefits swoop queried") which devoted two column inches to the protests of "civil rights campaigners". But when they did come out, the facts of the civil rights issues spoke for themselves and the other side was eventually heard, though only in the small-circulation weeklies and the specialist press and TV (*New Society*: "The tale in the Sting", September 9; *LAG Bulletin*: "Oxford court 'disgrace' – say solicitors", October 1982; *Community Care* editorial, September 9; *Social Work Today*: "Tenants' frights", September 14; BBC *Grapevine*: "The Oxfraud Incident", October 28; NCCL's *Rights*: "Operation Major: The facts behind the headlines", October 1982).

The criminal claimant

"Teams of swindlers"

Once the moment had passed for reporting the actual event, the media followed a classic pattern in such cases and moved on to generalisations, eager to demonstrate that "fiddling" was not confined to Oxford. Bands of highly organised "fiddlers", it was claimed, are moving round the country conning 'our' money out of the DHSS. Connections were immediately made between Oxford and the behaviour of homeless claimants at large. "Investigators" implied to the press that claimants were working double – or even triple –claims. London's *The Standard* explained: "So all a down-and-out has to do is to claim his daily benefit in one place, make arrangements for an accommodation address in another (perhaps paying a commission to the owner of the house concerned) and then claim the full weekly benefit." ("Time to unravel the great benefit shambles", September 6).

One man allegedly described to *The Sun* (September 4) "how the cheats can make three draws a week using their own name and then false identities to claim triple benefit". This anonymous man said: " 'It's easy to pick up £150 a week with very few question asked' ". He described keeping a network of addresses of "safe" houses all over the country, paying "backhanders" to landlords, and "arriving by the coachload where payouts are the highest".

On the same day, the *Daily Mail* ran a story apparently generated by the DHSS entitled, "Teams of swindlers are moving around country". The *Mail* identified eight categories of "fiddle" and gave unsubstantiated examples of each. They presented a riotous assembly of husbands skulking in wardrobes in order for their wives to claim they are unsupported; single mothers purporting to live alone when in reality they're kept by boyfriends or parents; strikers who get 'cap money' from their mates while drawing benefit; taxi drivers, waitresses and father christmases [sic] who carry on claiming even though they're employed; "penniless paupers" who get single payments to pay bills while running a savings account ("one claimant even had foreign accounts"); married women who claim under their former names (known, in the trade, apparently, as "Maidens' money") and "walking invalids – they say they can't work because of damaged lungs, dizzy spells, headaches, bad backs and even partial paralysis. Yet they are really in perfect health".

This cartoon, published in *The Sun* on September 4, became the subject of a complaint to the Press Council. In reality four black people were arrested out of the total 283. Two were released without charge, one had his case dismissed and one was convicted.

Scrounger myths

Amid the backwash of generalisation, *The Sun* (September 3) unearthed two scrounger stories with all the obligatory ingredients. One told of the Leeds man who drew £3,000 in benefit while his wife, "a top class stripper", earned "over £14,000". The other concerned a "trickster" from Nottingham who "swindled £13,000 by claiming she was an unmarried mum", when all the time she was driving "an £8,000 sports car". *The Standard* (September 6) informed its readers that "the deceptions practised by false claimants are diverse and ingenious". It related the incomprehensible case of an "Irish gipsy couple" who impersonated fellow Irishmen in order to obtain "birth certificates which they then used to make false claims worth £18,000". The *Mail* (September 4) contributed a tale of "seven Irishmen" who collected "legitimate handouts in Bedford on Thursday mornings before travelling to Cambridge for afternoon payments". The racist connection was taken further by *The Sun* (September 4), which published a cartoon showing that out of 12 'scroungers' sailing past the magistrates on a conveyor belt, four were black. In reality, only four out of 283 people arrested in Operation Major were black; two were released without charge, one had his case dismissed and one was convicted.

Interestingly, each of these stories links 'scroungers' with another familiar scapegoat – a stripper, an "unmarried mum", seven Irishmen, Irish gipsies and blacks. *The Sun* additionally claimed on September 3 that "official statistics show that dole fiddlers are not workshy – they claim benefits while holding down jobs". If "official statistics" could actually show this, there would be no need for fraud investigators to investigate it.

Justifying Operation Major

The media had thus brought all the stock characters and myths into play. The usual next step is to foment moral panic at the outrages apparently uncovered, thus licensing a full scale and punitive response. It was in this direction that the media went next. In reporting the so-called ramifications throughout the country, the press achieved a curious paradox whereby this unique event, upon which they had all fastened with such zeal, was suddenly portrayed as a commonplace occurrance – though little (if any) evidence was adduced to support the fact.

The tip of the iceberg

Oxford's claimants were allegedly travelling from "Blackpool, Birmingham, Coventry, Leicester and Leeds". Variations on this list were universally reported. *The Guardian* added Derby and *The Sun* Manchester and London. These cities may certainly have featured on the claimants' particulars, but there is nothing incriminating about that. Specifically, the press implied that claimants were signing on in Leeds, then coming to Oxford to make a second claim. In fact two people were discovered to be making double claims, but the idea was implanted in the minds of the public that it was happening on a grand scale. An early allegation that people were turning up to claim in taxis was dropped by the BBC.

From a police prosecutor, the press learned that people were allegedly coming "from all over the country mainly for the specific purpose of defrauding the DHSS" (Radio 4 *News*, midnight, September 2; *Daily Express*, September 3). This information was corroborated by a "Ministry Investigator" who said that people were coming from the West Midlands and the North West and that "this was just a start, the tip of the iceberg" (*Daily Express* September 3). BBC Radio was only slightly more cautious: "while no one was prepared to say that Oxford is the tip of the iceberg, no one could say that similar frauds were not happening elsewhere" (Radio 4 *News*, 6 pm, September 3).

The 'tip-of-the-iceberg' theme was taken up with alacrity over the weekend of September 4/5. It was posed by Tory MP Jill Knight and reported in the *Mail* (September 4). *The Times* ran a story entitled "Benefit frauds 'rampant' in lodging houses", which drew on CHAR's material about racketeering private landlords but quoted DHSS officials "all over the country" saying that "frauds based on fake addresses were not uncommon" (September 4). "Officers have now learned that similar full-scale deceptions are going on in other cities," reported the *Daily Star* (September 4). "One town has been labelled 'the softest touch in the land' ". " 'One place makes this operation in Oxford look very small,' said a senior detective" (*Mirror* September 4), "Detectives have established that similar rackets have been operating in other parts of the country" (*Sunday Telegraph* September 5). Once again, the source of all these stories was the police and the DHSS.

How many fiddlers?

Several of the national dailies fastened on to Sir Derek Rayner's study for the Department of Employment and the DHSS and reported (as did a *Daily Telegraph* headline on September 7) that "One in 12 dole claims 'are fraudulent' " (or, as *The Standard* would have it, "one in eight" (September 6)). The Rayner study in fact makes it clear that the exact amount of benefit fraud is unknown. The estimate was actually based on two particular fraud drives being conducted at the time by special investigators, but the Government responded to Rayner by saying that "There must be considerable doubt about the accuracy of the team's estimate". The *Telegraph* refused to print two letters, one from the National Association of Probation Officers, the other from the Child Poverty Action Group, correcting the misleading statement – in fact it devoted a leader to the subject – while *The Sun* actually used Rayner's estimate to extrapolate a figure of 200,000 scroungers (September 3). The *Express* Opinion column, "Counting the cost" (September 4), asked, "How much is the whole country losing? £100m? £200m? £300m?". *The Sun* ran the headline, "Dole swindles cost £400m" (September 3). The *Mail* (September 4) put it at £500 million.

Deterring claimants

"The DHSS believes that radio, TV and newspaper publicity given to Thursday's arrests will deter others planning to make false claims for b&b allowances", reported the *Sunday Telegraph* on September 5. The DHSS entered into the spirit of scroungerphobia with enthusiasm, and the department must have known, as it fed the press with stories, that it was not just "fiddlers" who would be deterred from claiming. None of the newspapers except the *Morning Star* (September 3) mentioned that some "£500 million" of benefit goes unclaimed each year, though the point did come out on the BBC TV *9 o'clock News* (September 2) when newsreader Michael Buerk quoted the Claimants' Union saying that police and DHSS tactics would inhibit even more people from making rightful claims.

In the wider justification of DHSS fraud detection (and in particular Specialist Claims Control), *The Times* (September 4) pointed out that £217 million in benefits had been saved in 1981/82. *The Sun* (September 3) claimed that £170 million had been saved by 2,250 investigators. *The Standard* (September 6) put the number of investigators at 500. In fact, £171 million was officially 'saved' by 5,640 staff in 1980/81 and £217 million by 5,500 staff in 1981/82 (*Hansard*, July 29 1982, col 667). But these figures are open to serious doubt.

Mr Big

The media sought a culprit – and were rewarded with the police assertion that behind the claimants lurked organised crime.

By pursuing a scapegoat they were deflected from any concern with the processes and problems behind the events. This theme surfaced early with the announcement by ITN that "one report said [the fraud] was masterminded by a Mr Big who took a cut from all those collecting money" (September 2, *News at 5.45*). The *Daily Star* spoke of Mr Big "Masterminding the plot" (September 3) while the *Express* (September 4) had him "getting a cut from wanderers coming in from all over the country". The *Mirror* reported (September 4) that "detectives had been told Mr Big took £100,000 in backhanders during the past year". This information came from Cronin's 'agent', who had by this time given a detailed statement to the police (see p. 62). Once again, the police themselves must have been the source of the information, but they evidently chose to withhold the fact that the alleged "Mr Big" was not in fact a social security 'scrounger' himself, but one of the landlords. When Parliamentary Under Secretary Tony Newton was interviewed by Richard Whitmore on BBC TV *News* (September 3, 1 pm), he asked if the fraud was being managed by "organised gangs", but the Minister replied that he believed "individual action" to be the greater part of it.

Putting the other side

Implicating the landlords and the DHSS

ITN switched its emphasis to the landlords on September 3 and on the 4th *The Guardian* and *The Times* quoted CHAR on the subject of landlord exploitation of the homeless. Then, on September 7, the *Oxford Mail* led with a story entitled "The Greedy Landlords", based on what one of the solicitors had said in court – "Solicitor tells of £50,000 fortunes". This story was picked up by the *Daily Telegraph* and *The Guardian* (September 8) but the tabloids ignored it. ITN (September 3) and the *Daily Telegraph* (September 11) ran interviews with the two landlords, Patel and Cronin, respectively. Both protested their innocence, but Cronin admitted to an annual turnover of £100,000 and profit of £28,000.

The Guardian, The Times and ITN (September 3 and 4) also quoted CHAR on the responsibility of the DHSS, while the *Morning Star* (September 4) and *The World This Weekend* (September 5) brought out the allegation that the DHSS had "known of the fraud for seven years".

Quoting the 'other side'

The police had had a long time to prepare their press statements and anyone with a different point of view from theirs was clearly at a serious disadvantage when it came to putting it across. Initial demonstrations by the Claimants' Union were mentioned by ITN and BBC TV *News* (September 2) and by *The Guardian, The Times* and *The Sun*, (September 3). The *Express* quoted a member of the Claimants' Union saying that the operation was "absolutely horrifying" – a quote the paper used against the claimants in its Opinion column the following day: "In this way, morality is turned on its head and those who uphold the law are made out to be persecutors; the culprits become the victims. . ."

By the weekend, with ITN's Friday evening coverage of CHAR's position on landlords, interviews with members of the Claimants' Union on BBC TV *9 o'clock News, The World This Weekend* and the small *Sunday Times* piece on the 5th, the 'other side' was starting to be heard. But it was no match for the PR triumph already pulled off by the police.

The cost of the exercise

The Guardian and the *Sunday Times* (September 5) quoted the claimants and Oxfordshire County Councillor Julian Jacottet querying the cost of Operation Major, a point which also came in up the interviews on *The World This Weekend. The Guardian* and the *Morning Star* reported that it costs £160 a week to keep someone in prison (the current figure is actually £177). The *Telegraph* (September 8) quoted the Society of Civil and Public Servants saying that Operation Major could have been avoided if claimants had been properly interviewed when they were first seen. On BBC *Nationwide (South East)* (September 3), Ruth Lister of the Child Poverty Action Group was encouraged to compare Operation Major unfavourably with the Inland Revenue's less spectacular, more cost-effective investigations into tax fraud. The *Oxford Mail* published a piece on the £21,000 DHSS cost. But nowhere in the national media has anyone questioned the £1½ million "savings" Operation Major is supposed to have achieved (see pp.24-25).

Inadequate benefits

Most of the press quoted the benefit levels and the difference between the residential rate of £67.20 and the 'NFA' [no fixed address] rate of £18.60. *The Guardian, Mirror, Express, Sun, Times* and BBC TV quoted the figures without comment, but the *Telegraph* leader (September 7) surprisingly referred to the NFA rate as "grindingly little" and called for more money. *The Standard* (September 6) said: "To such a man, the difference [between the rates] can be the difference between starving and eating. The temptation to fiddle is strong. . .'

Comparisons with tax dodging

Once the focus of reporting had moved away from the event itself, it concentrated on setting Operation Major in the context of other incidences of social security fraud. But it did not, by and large, compare it to other frauds on the public purse. The *Express* Opinion column (September 4) maintained that "it is taxpayers who are being cheated when men and women make false claims. . . the fiddlers are thieves". But it ventured no estimate of how much tax dodgers cost the country each year – possibly because the two are quite distinct from each other in the public consciousness. As Peter Golding points out, swindling the tax man shows flair. The money is 'theirs' – the bureaucrats'. With benefit fraud, the money suddenly becomes 'ours'.

Only the *Morning Star* in its editorial "The tax dodgers sting us all" (September 4) drew the comparison, and quoted an estimate of £4,000 million a year lost through tax evasion. *The Guardian*'s report of September 3 alluded to tax evasion in a quote from the Claimants' Union, but no other newspaper appears to have made the link.

In contrast to the priority given to publicity in Operation Major, a case to reach the Oxford courts just one month later passed almost unnoticed. It concerned allegations of tax fraud involving the directors of the Bear Hotel, Woodstock, which is "by appointment to his Grace the Duke of Marlborough". To get bail, the father and son directors had to produce joint sureties of £100,000 plus an additional £100,000 cash security. Their passports were taken away and strict reporting conditions to the police were imposed. The case was reported in the *Oxford Mail* on October 22. But only just. There was no press notification for this story, as there had been for Operation Major; the police were not involved, and the *Oxford Mail* would not have found out about it but for an informal tip-off in the pub.

Another story contemporary with the Oxford arrests to invite a comparison of press coverage is the suspension, in October 1982, of Lloyds underwriter Ian Postgate following revelations about irregular accounting practices involving millions of dollars within the Alexander Howden Group. Peter Golding compared coverage of the two stories in the *Mirror, Star, Sun, Express* and *Mail* and found that the Oxford arrests attracted 309 column inches while the Lloyds story filled only 14 (*The Sun, Star* and *Mirror* ignored it altogether).

Aftermath

The 'Sting' 's press life was short. *The Guardian* was the only newspaper to follow up any aspect of it apart from the initial toll of prison sentences (though the *Telegraph* painstakingly printed all the sentences). At first glance, the reasons for the story's sudden demise are puzzling. There was no major issue to drive it off the news pages: *The Sun* and the *Star* progressed to a bank raid in Clacton; the *Telegraph* to events in Poland. The next major event was the TUC Conference. The fact is that having defined and reported the incident as a 'crime', there could be no logical follow-up except the sentences. With a flurry of reports on "The final Sting as 16 fiddlers get jailed" (*Daily Star*, September 7), the press retired, its duty done. A press release issued by NAPO* on the 7th received scant attention. The reporters didn't stick around to record that when the innocent pleas came to court, most cases were being dismissed for lack of evidence. And, with the exception of *The Guardian* (September 25) and the *Oxford Mail* (September 24), they ignored Thames Valley's statement to the Police Authority that one of its officers was about to be investigated for alleged fabrication of evidence (an announcement which coincided with the publication of an article on the subject by the *New Statesman*). The Oxford press – *Mail, Times* and *Star* – reported the outcome of the court cases and events leading to the DHSS strike with increasing sympathy for the claimants. The *Oxford Mail* eventually called for an enquiry into Operation Major.

To sum up, the media may be criticised almost as much for what it failed to say as for the nature of what it did report. There was virtually no discussion of the NFA rate or the benefit system, and no explanation of the fact that but for the claimants' homelessness they would have been entitled to the benefit they had 'fiddled'. Where material was used about the discomfort of those under arrest, it was quoted without comment or follow-up. No major newspaper, radio or TV programme pursued the civil liberties angle. The whole story dropped so rapidly from the news that no follow-ups set the record straight after the first flush of distorted images ("teams of swindlers", *et al*) and exaggerated claims (£1½ million). There was no investigation into the *real* savings or costs of the operation; no account of the conduct of the courts (except in *LAG Bulletin*); questioning of the parts played by the landlords, or of the underlying housing crisis.

---

* National Association of Probation Officers.

4 THE LANDLORDS

Oxford's private landlords

With its acute shortage of permanent private rented accommodation, Oxford is a city of opportunity for profiteering boarding house landlords. Single homeless claimants are an attractive group of clients for such landlords because the profits to be made from them are enormous. Lodging charges are already high compared with fair rents, and can be further boosted by crowding several people into one room. The payments are guaranteed because the money comes from the government. The condition of the property, the level of overcrowding and the standards of cleanliness go virtually unchecked by local authorities because the single homeless have no status. And the residents are licensees – they have no security of tenure, and almost no rights whatsoever.

How much accommodation?

Apart from the two named landlords at the centre of Operation Major, there are half a dozen more who cater for the single homeless in Oxford. Numbers of beds in these smaller establishments are thought not to exceed 15 each, even with overcrowding taken into account. In one or two of them the standard is higher than at

Jeremiah Cronin, landlord.

Cronin's; in the rest it is similar, or worse. A claimant who stayed at Cronin's was an ex-resident at a place in Cowley Road, where people slept five to a room with more in a caravan and a tiled shed in the garden. Nevertheless it appears that no other landlord in the city is making profits on the scale of Cronin and Patel out of accommodation of as low a quality – though with the acute shortage of housing, none of these landlords is exactly out of pocket. Taking all these landlords into account, it can be roughly estimated that in a typical week the Oxford DHSS could be paying out £7,500 to private landlords for single homeless people alone – about £390,000 a year.

Cronin and Patel

But it is Cronin and Patel who are most closely involved with the Oxford benefits frauds, since theirs were the addresses which the police claimed were being fraudulently used by claimants. Both landlords became witnesses for the prosecution.

Haribhai Patel runs at least six houses, including 7 and 59 Western Road, 1 Iffley Road (owned by his son), 169 Iffley Road and 31 and 34 Marlborough Road. The exact number of beds used by homeless claimants in these houses is unknown, but Oxford Housing Aid Centre estimates that it is over 70. Patel is not himself resident at any of the houses but lives with his son in Harberton Mead, Headington.

The four houses run by Jeremiah Cronin at 131, 133, 137 and 141 Iffley Road, Cowley, are known collectively as the Nanford Guest House. According to Cronin's police statement, they hold approximately 75 people (with up to four sharing a room). The local DHSS was apparently aware that 20-30 people above this official maximum were living there. Cronin, an ex-British Leyland worker, runs the Nanford Guest House with the help of his two sons. According to residents, there is never an empty bed.

How much do they legally make?

A few days after the arrests, 20 beds were moved out of Cronin's – representing a loss of £840 a week potential income. On the basis of his police statement that his boarding house has 75 beds, his potential annual income is £163,800 (75 beds @ £42/week). His turnover is more than £3,000 a week. Cronin, who owns a £100,000 house in Sunningwell, Berks., admitted annual profits of £28,000 on a £100,000 turnover to the *Daily Telegraph* (September 11), but people who know his establishment feel this to be a conservative estimate. Patel, whose weekly rate recently rose to £45.50, presumably makes a similar amount.

Life at Cronin and Patel's

In court, ex-residents repeatedly gave the overcrowding, the poor conditions and the lack of security as their reasons for leaving Cronin's. The unlucky ones were housed in the 'annexe' – a damp asbestos shed in the back garden. One man said: "I used to go out some days and when I came back he had put someone else in my bed". This double-booking of beds was a common complaint. A man who went away for the weekend came back to find that someone had been sleeping in his bed and had urinated on the sheets, which were not changed. Mike Hall of the Oxford Cyrenians describes conditions at 137 Iffley Road as appalling. "I visited a basement room where four old men were sleeping. They were using a large baked bean tin as a chamber pot." Anthony Kelleher found himself in a room with an incontinent man who urinated on the floor. The floor was never cleaned.

A current resident of Cronin's describes what it's like to live there:–

"I discovered that the place was full, so I had to wait before going there. I was eventually given a note for the DHSS stating that I could live at 137 Iffley Road at the cost of £6 a night. This got me a voucher for seven nights and a giro of £25.20, and I went back and presented the voucher to Cronin. One of his workers then took me to a room in the basement of 131 Iffley Road. There was four beds in this room, one of which was to be mine. Besides the beds there was a wardrobe and a wash-hand basin. Adjoining this room was a box-room approximately six and a half feet square and that had a further two beds in it. Later I realized that this was how things were in all four of Cronin's houses. In the three basement rooms at 131 Iffley Road there were eight beds, so the basement of this house alone was bringing in £336 a week.

"Next morning, on waking, I found that only one towel had been provided for the six men in my room and the box-room next door. We washed and shaved and went up for breakfast, where we found a small dining room with three tables. The room could only sit 16 men at a time, so we waited. Eventually we were able to sit down and were served with cornflakes, and bacon, egg and beans. This breakfast had been fried before 7 o'clock and kept on a hot plate, and in this manner the egg gained the consistency of rubber and the bacon was so crisp that when you touched it with a fork it shattered. Breakfast was from seven till nine, so the food had plenty of time to bake.

"Later we discovered some of the other drawbacks of Cronin's. There were men who were skippering there because they would not pay the rent. One man had lived there and retained the front door key: he used to come in at night and pull blankets of people's beds and sleep on the floor. In the end, we got fed up with this and threw him bodily out of the house. Doors into rooms were never locked and with only one wardrobe for all of us to keep our clothes in, things had a habit of disappearing and were never seen again.

"The staff who worked for Cronin were all men drawing benefits from the DHSS, so Cronin was able to get away with paying very little for the job. Beds would be left unchanged and in some cases a man just moving in would be given a bed whose sheets had not been changed after the last man left.

"All of Cronin's houses were badly in need of repair. Beds with legs knocked off were propped up on bricks. Bannisters were loose and could be lifted off the stairs. Doors wouldn't shut and floorboards were loose. He seemed to have bought

Paul Gateley and John Meiklejohn inside Cronin's boarding house. The room is less than six feet wide.

Martin Stott

oddments of wallpaper to decorate the rooms – you'd get four different patterns on a wall.

"It was not unusual for men to go out for an evening and come back to find someone sleeping in their bed. When they complained Cronin would say he thought the bed was empty and would then move the man to another room. This so called 'mistake' was made even when the original resident had left some of his possessions on the bed. It showed that Cronin had no idea who was staying in his houses and no interest in providing accommodation – beyond making all the money he could."

Oxford Housing Aid Centre makes a clear distinction between Cronin's boarding house and the various hostels run by Mr Patel. Patel's, they say, is in a "higher league" with regard to standards of cleanliness and lack of overcrowding.

But it seems life is made unpleasant for residents at Patel's in other ways. They have to be off the premises from 8.30 am till 5.30 pm. This rule was not relaxed even for a disabled woman, or in the heavy winter snow of 1981/82 (though on the very worst days they were allowed back inside an hour early). Residents complain of uneatable breakfasts, stringent rules and erratic behaviour on the part of the proprietors, including the eviction of a pregnant woman when she made a complaint and the splitting of a husband and wife into separate rooms. One claimant was allegedly accused of breaking into an electricity meter – until it was pointed out that the meter had been by-passed and was not in use.

The landlords' relationship with the statutory authorities

Most of the statutory agencies have been referring clients to Cronin's and Patel's for a number of years. The Council's Housing Aid Centre, the DHSS and Social Services use the private boarding houses because they say they have no alternative. The Probation Service has been using Cronin's for 10 years. Cronin's is also well-known to the courts, who have asked probation officers to refer homeless defendants there. With the exception of September 2, 137 Iffley Road has always been acceptable as a bail address.

Though they continue to send people there, neither the DHSS nor the Council has carried out inspections of the premises on any regular basis. Prior to September 2, the DHSS had not inspected for months – staff shortages having necessitated even greater lapses in standard visiting times than should have been the case. As one housing worker put it: "I know this is not a substitute for offering people decent accommodation, but at least they have a roof over their heads and get slightly more benefit than the £18.60 under the NFA [no fixed address] rate. Agencies use Cronin's out of sheer desperation."

The reason which is always given by councils and statutory agencies – not just in Oxford but wherever this type of accommodation is used – for not reducing the numbers of beds or enforcing decent standards is that there is nowhere else for the single homeless to go. This is true, of course, and the 'professionals' are in a constant dilemma about continuing to operate a corrupt, expensive system when they know that what's needed is a major initiative – a radical re-allocation and input of public money – to provide decent housing for the homeless.

But the professionals' sense of helplessness has lulled them into believing there is no alternative. It seems to have deprived them of the will to take the limited steps that *are* open to them – to enforce minimum standards of repair, hygiene and fire safety and to limit excessive overcrowding (though legislation on overcrowding is hopelessly inadequate).

These powers lie with council environmental health departments, but the powers are discretionary and in many parts of the country they are not used. Oxford's environmental health officers were not prepared to comment on whether or not they have inspected the premises of Cronin and Patel, but according to Cronin they have not. The Oxford Fire Service would not give information about whether or not it has issued fire certificates to Cronin's or any other establishment. It would say only that certificates "have been issued in some cases but not all".

The Nanford Guest House, 137-141 Iffley Road, Cowley.

Were the landlords involved in the fraud?

Patel operates a system of 'deposits', exacting a payment of £6 from any claimant seeking the verification letter which will prove to the DHSS that he or she is staying at one of his houses. Claimants exchange the letter for a voucher which they then return to Patel. But they say the 'deposit' is unreturnable.

Cronin employed an 'agent' at 137 Iffley Road, whose work making breakfast and serving at table was allegedly supplemented by more unusual duties. This man was arrested by the police on September 2 and made a five-page statement to them in which he said that Cronin had shown him how to write letters to the DHSS verifying that a claimant was staying at his address. This enabled the claimant to get a higher rate of benefit than the NFA rate. The vouchers were then bought from the claimant for £5 or £10, said the agent, and cashed for £42 (the value of the voucher to the landlord). He described another of his duties as receiving money from claimants outside the post office as they cashed their weekly giros – money which he, and his predecessor, had handed on to the landlord.

He further alleged that after three or four weeks Cronin would demand more payments from claimants if they "wanted to keep this address going", under threat of disclosure to the DHSS that they were not actually staying at Iffley Road. The agent said that a good 20 people had been threatened by the landlord in his presence.

This statement was in part corroborated on September 16 by a letter from Oxford Cyrenians' ex-chairwoman Alison Harris. The letter, published in the *Oxford Star*, said:–

Fiver for DHSS fraud

May I tell you how the system of defrauding the DHSS worked? . . . While at [the boarding house], an associate of the landlord would tell the man that next week, instead of the voucher, the DHSS would give him the cash (£42) if he signed a form saying his "situation had not changed". He could then either pay the rent to a landlord and continue to stay there, in extreme overcrowded squalor. Or he could give £5 to the associate (who waited outside the DHSS), and who would then tell the DHSS the lodger still occupied the room; and thus the man might keep the rest for himself.

Many homeless people, in summertime especially, found it was more bearable to sleep in the open, with the extra

money, than return to such a boarding house. Oxford is so short of accommodation that, for many such people, there is seldom any other choice. . .
I would not condone anyone's dishonesty. The fact that these boarding houses were said to be so overcrowded indicates that many people did resist the temptation to defraud the DHSS. But do you not think it wrong that the man who, over the years, defrauded the DHSS out of far the greater amount of money, should not also be called to account?

How private landlords make profits throughout the country

In every city, landlords are gathering huge profits from exploiting homeless people's need for a place to stay. They accommodate a steady supply of newcomers referred to them by council social services and housing departments, probation offices and the DHSS, secure in the knowledge that the rent will be regular and few questions asked about what goes on behind the front door. Frequently these 'hotels' are dirty, overcrowded and well below minimum standards for environmental health and fire safety. Some

1 Iffley Road, Cowley. This house is run by Haribhai Patel for homeless people.

have been judged by environmental health officers to be a statutory nuisance, or even unfit for human habitation. Yet nothing is done to improve them and public money keeps pouring into the landlords' pockets.

This exploitation is rarely challenged. The homeless residents who complain can be quickly put back on to the streets as they have virtually no security of tenure. When it is challenged, usually by an outside group, many authorities have preferred to avoid their responsibility than acknowledge their complicity in maintaining the racket. In January 1978 CHAR, the Campaign for Single Homeless People, complained to Leeds City Housing Department about the appalling standards and fire risks in the Grove Hostel, a lodging house for 53 men. The Assistant Director of Housing said: "We believe that to try and substantially improve the facilities and amenities at the Grove Hostel would make it unacceptable as a place of shelter to the type of men who at present avail themselves of its shelter." Two men died and eleven more were injured in a fire which gutted the hostel only three months later.

A report by Leicester CHAR in 1980 identified two landlords who made substantial profits from lodging houses which offered overcrowded rooms, "filthy lino, unhygienic toilets, soiled sheets and blankets smelling of sweat and cracked and damp plasterwork". The owner of the lodging house, Mr A.S. Biddles, was estimated to make about £70,000 per year. CHAR calculated that the DHSS was paying out some £½ million each year to the owners of the city's 24 worst lodging houses, providing about 350 beds.

In 1979 Shelter's magazine *Roof* investigated lodging houses in Birmingham. In the Palm Court Hotel, Moseley, Mrs Knight housed over 100 people, 89 of whom were either "mentally subnormal or mentally unbalanced". Mrs Knight received a weekly income of £2,500 from the DHSS and employed residents as cleaners and kitchen assistants for £4 per week. The City Environmental Health Officer sent Mrs Knight a list of defects requiring attention, but he commented to Shelter: "this will be costly and it is somewhat difficult to see how Mrs Knight will be able to meet the cost out of her present income".

Mr Biddles and Mrs Knight are not exceptional. Throughout London there are 'hotels' and 'lodging houses' raking in money from the DHSS and local authorities for providing accommodation well below standard. Rowton Hotels, who have made enormous profits from homeless men for almost 100 years are now pulling out because of pressure to improve their hostels.

5 THE DHSS

How the benefits system encourages abuse

Disparity in benefit levels

Supplementary benefit (SB) is a means-tested benefit which is intended to provide a basic minimum for all those unable to gain an income from another source. The total amount allowed for expenditure on weekly needs (apart from housing) is the scale rate. Each year, in November, the scale rates are increased to keep pace with inflation – on September 2 a single householder would have received £23.25 (for an analysis of how he or she might be expected to spend this money, see Appendix 2), and a claimant living in bed and breakfast received £25.20 for meals and personal expenses.

But there is a disparity between the rate of benefit paid to claimants with accommodation and the rate paid to claimants of no fixed address (NFA). Homeless claimants receive only £18.60 a week *in total.* This rate is often paid in daily instalments of £2.65. Over the last couple of years its real value has been eroded, since in 1980 the rate did not increase at all. This was because the method for calculating a homeless person's benefit was changed: if the previous system were still in use (the weekly total of a boarder's meals allowances) homeless claimants would receive £23.80 a week. The Secretary of State for Social Services (then Patrick Jenkin MP) defended this cut by saying:

> "It was felt that a non-householder would have cause to feel aggrieved if he saw that a person could get more actual cash in hand by being homeless (sometimes by choice) than by contributing towards the cost of a household and accepting the attendant responsibilities."

This reveals the implied hierarchy of benefit rates. To maintain differentials, the DHSS meanly pared down the lowest, when there is a need for *all* rates to be increased.

A person of no fixed abode receives no money for housing costs because there are none. Yet clearly there is a need to meet the higher cost of food necessitated by the homeless having to use cafes because they have nowhere to cook for themselves. In this, their situation is similar to boarders whose lodgings or hostels do not provide meals. For such people the standard payment (until November 1982) was £1.25 each for lunch and dinner and 90p for breakfast. According to the rate issued to boarders, it would be inconsistent for the daily rate of benefit for a homeless claimant to have been less than £3.40, giving a weekly rate of £23.80 for food alone.

The weekly amount of benefit, however, does not just have to meet food. Regulation 4 of the SB Requirements Regulations sets out what this amount of money is intended to buy, effectively stating that the benefit is meant to cover normal expenditure on day to day living, except for housing costs such as rent:–

> "Including in particular food, household fuel, the purchase, cleaning, repair and replacement of clothing and footwear, normal travel costs, weekly laundry costs, miscellaneous household expenses such as toilet articles, cleaning materials, window cleaning and replacement of small household goods. . . and leisure and amenity items such as television licence and rental, newspapers, confectionery and tobacco."

Homeless people will obviously not have to meet the miscellaneous household expenses, but they will spend money on clothes, footwear, travel costs, and 'leisure and amenity' items. Some of these expenses (eg washing clothes) may be greater for someone without a home because of the necessity to use public facilities, such as launderettes. Even from a cursory analysis of the costs additional to the purchase of food, it is clear that the rate of £18.60 requires immediate amendment. Boarders receive an amount for personal expenses (£7.70 in 1981/2). Their needs in this respect must be similar to those of the homeless.

In Oxford, £2.65 won't even pay for two meals a day, let alone breakfast, cups of tea or coffee, cigarettes, bus fares, clothes... And all this when claimants are forced by their very homelessness to spend their life on the streets, which is much more costly than staying at home. The pitiful inadequacy of the NFA rate means that the homeless remain dependent on charitable handouts, while the disparity between the rates actually invites fraud. This situation is aggravated by the reluctance of DHSS officers to make extra 'single payments' (to which claimants are theoretically entitled) – even when a payment for travel or clothes for a job interview might actually enable the claimant to stop claiming. Many of those arrested in Operation Major are actively looking for work, but their poverty helps disqualify them from finding it. One man told the court during the Operation Major hearings that he had spent a night in a toilet in order to save his rent money for the bus fare for a job interview.

Harassment of NFA claimants

The NFA allowance, small as it is, is difficult to get, both in Oxford and elsewhere. It is mandatory (SB Requirements Regulations, Reg. 10 and Schedule 2 Para. 4) but in some areas local offices simply don't pay it. Many who would be eligible for it don't claim, partly because of the common belief that benefit cannot be claimed without a permanent address and partly because of the delays and difficulties which people encounter when they do try to claim.

In the Oxford DHSS office, where shortcomings of the system have been exacerbated by cuts in staffing, NFA claimants are frequently 'mucked about'. Two 16-year-olds, who had been released without charge on September 2, returned to the South Oxford Middle School the next day – as instructed – to collect their benefit. They were sent to the DHSS office at Marston Road, but when they got there it was closed. They were then told they would have to wait for their money until the following Wednesday – five days. They were literally penniless and homeless. A member of the Claimants' Union contacted Oxford Social Services on their behalf, and was told by the duty social worker that the DHSS had said all those who should have been paid on Friday night *were* paid. Various other possibilities were suggested to her by the Claimants' Union (including their eligibility as 'vulnerable' because of their youth under section 1 of the Housing (Homeless Persons) Act

1977) but her only suggestion was that they spend the night at the police station – something which, after their experiences of the previous day, they were understandably loath to do. As it was, they had no alternative but to wait the five days – as did all NFA claimants in Oxford from September 2 onwards.

One point to emerge from the court hearings is that the level of NFA payments, and the fact they are paid daily, actually perpetuate claimants' homelessness. A bed at the Salvation Army hostel costs about £5, but the only way to get in is to turn up with money in advance. NFA claimants receiving benefit on a daily basis never have £5 at a time – let alone enough money to get a permanent room in the private sector. The DHSS can make a payment for rent in advance, but the power is discretionary and the money will be recouped over the following week. In practice, rent in advance is extremely difficult to get. Deposits are also practically impossible to come by: Regulation 14 of the Single Payment Regulations states that you may qualify for a payment to cover a deposit – provided you've got the tenancy first. In practice, you can't secure a tenancy until you hand over the deposit.

The housing allowance

In order to get a reasonable rate of benefit, a claimant needs a permanent address. The address must be certified by the landlord, who may even be empowered to cash claimants' giros. Many landlords, including some in Oxford, allegedly charge a fee – say, £5 – for a letter to the DHSS verifying a claimant's address.

The maximum size of the housing allowance paid by the DHSS can be restricted under Requirements Regulation 9(4) to an amount estimated "as representing a reasonable weekly charge for full board and lodging... of no more than suitable standard". In practice this maximum is fixed annually by each local office relative to the rates charged by the local monopoly private landlords. But the landlords quickly adopt the maximum payable – £42 at the time of Operation Major – as their minimum charge, because that is what they know they can get out of the DHSS. Some even raise the rate slightly above this maximum (as in the case of Mr Patel, whose weekly rate has since risen to £45.50), thereby eating into claimants' living allowances if they still wish to stay there. The effect of this is to keep forcing up the local maximum. In that respect, local landlords actually dictate to the DHSS.

This practice would not be possible if the DHSS inspected the premises and exercised some authority over the facilities to be

Martin Stott

Entrance to the temporary benefit office set up by the police and DHSS at the South Oxford Middle School.

provided in return for charging maximum rates. It could be further controlled if the Council's Environmental Health Department used its powers to enforce housing standards. But the Department does not. Up to two years ago, the DHSS did carry out precautionary checks on addresses, like Cronin's, which were designated 'unsafe'. But first a procedural change from central government lengthened the standard interval between visits to a year and then, in 1982, staff shortages at the local office became so acute that visits were virtually discontinued altogether (until, strangely enough, the week following the arrests, when there was a sudden rash of inspections). Ironically, therefore, concern to get value for money is a luxury the DHSS cannot afford.

The DHSS was aware of abuse

When Mike Hall of the Oxford Cyrenians said that the DHSS had known about the 'fiddles' for at least seven years, there were outright denials from Meurig Jones, manager of the local office. Mike Hall alleges that he had brought the matter to the DHSS's attention several times over the years. In her letter to the *Oxford Star* (September 16) one-time chairwoman of the Cyrenians, Alison Harris, wrote:–

I was chairman of Simon House from 1976 to 1979. On several occasions over the years the matter of these particular private boarding houses was discussed among our committee, and Michael Hall, the warden, told us that the DHSS had said they were unable to prevent the operation of this landlord, except by constantly sending round investigators to see that his lodgers were really there.

One committee member has more than once asked different officers of the DHSS what could be done to prevent it, to be told the same thing. I believe the DHSS has known of this landlord and his method of encouraging homeless people to defraud them, and has wanted to stop him, for many years.

Privately, senior officers at the DHSS have admitted that they did know of abuses some time ago but "had no proof". One staff member claims that she has been aware of the situation since 1974. An ex-staff member alleges that fraud investigators were working on Oxford's private landlords two years ago. A third staff member, who kept bringing the irregularities at Cronin's to her seniors' attention, was actually reprimanded for displaying lapses in judgement because she "kept going on about 137 Iffley Road".

Pressures on DHSS staffing.

The staff complement of 146 at the Oxford DHSS office has not increased since 1981, when the complement was established on a notional 'live' caseload of 12,742. The actual 'live' caseload in August 1981 was 16,599 and by August 1982 it had risen to 19,113. Yet because of a shift to fraud investigation work, the number of staff actually dealing with benefits has been reduced. The 15 per cent increase is in line with the increase in SB claimants nationally from 2,998,180 in July 1979 to 3,953,460 at the end of 1981 (*Hansard*, February 11 1982, col 461).

Throughout the summer of 1982, Oxford's SB staff warned their management that they were unable to cope with the increasing pressure of work. With staff holidays this pressure increased. Officers who were supposed to deal with only nine appointments a day were having to deal with twelve – plus four or so emergency interviews with urgent cases on top. It later transpired that orders had been given before September for an appointment system to be introduced for urgent cases, with priority for "local" people. However, this appointment system was postponed (see below). Staff knew nothing of this at the time, but were told that "something" would happen at the beginning of September which would solve all their problems. In the event, Operation Major created even more work for the hard-pressed staff since, in the

Jim Stanes

aftermath, people came flocking to the office to re-submit claims.

Immediately following the arrests, the DHSS local office introduced its appointment system. Some urgent cases were having to wait a week for an interview. "If we have a lot of people coming into town from other places then obviously they can't be dealt with ahead of the people from Oxford", DHSS manager Meurig Jones told the *Oxford Mail* on September 11. Clearly, he and his senior staff saw the appointment system as a means of driving homeless people out of Oxford – something they were literally prepared to do, since one benefit that *was* on offer was a travel warrant out of the area to DHSS-run resettlement centres at Camberwell and Newbury.

One man – an 'Oxford citizen' as it turned out – disclosed his change of address to the DHSS and consequently had to wait three weeks for his benefit (had he kept quiet he might have been charged with fraud). He was refused an urgent payment and told to come back in another week. A man with angina was also sent away for a week, both when he applied on his own for an urgent needs payment and when a probation officer and his solicitor approached the DHSS on his behalf. Members of the Claimants' Union accompanied him to the office in Marston Road and persuaded officers to bring his interview forward by two days – but still he was told he would have to sleep rough over the weekend. The Claimants' Union refused to leave the office until he had received his urgent needs payment. The police were called. The stress of all this brought on an angina attack and the claimant was taken to hospital on leaving the office. Before he went off in the ambulance his solicitor gave him some money; without it he would have had nothing.

The Claimants' Union responded to the new DHSS policy by lobbying the local office every day. But DHSS assistant manager Jane Mastroddi told them she had checked out the legal position on urgent payments: the office was within its rights not to grant an interview for up to two weeks, she said. She was correct. There is nothing in the Urgent Cases Regulations or elsewhere which requires a more immediate decision on an application for urgent need. The only duty in relation to the time within which benefit officers should make a decision on a claim for supplementary benefit is contained in Regulation 2 of the Determination of Questions Regulations. This states that decisions should be made "so far as practicable. . . within 14 days". The Claimants' Union was quick to point out that not even this was happening – some claimants were having to wait 14 weeks to have their cases processed – and this was confirmed by Ms Mastroddi.

But events in Oxford had taken a turn which was unacceptable to senior officers at DHSS national headquarters. On September 27 Parliamentary Under Secretary Tony Newton intervened with a ruling that all claimants in urgent need must be given an immediate interview where practicable. The Oxford staff agreed that this ruling was correct (particularly in view of section 27 of the Supplementary Benefit Act 1976, which says that the Secretary of State has a duty to ensure that decisions in local offices are taken in the claimants' best interests), but they were totally unable to operate it.

There was a walk-out at 3.50 on the 27th and the next day the staff voted unanimously to take industrial action. The Unions' demand for a total of 35 new posts was countered with a management offer of 10 regional reserves to ease the problem. The Unions rejected it. On September 29 the Oxford DHSS staff went on strike, and at the time of going to press the strike was still in progress – a considerable saving to the Government in unpaid benefits.

The part played in Operation Major by the DHSS

DHSS staff believe that although Operation Major was conceived by the police, it was planned jointly with the manager and two or three of the seven assistant managers of the Oxford DHSS office, who used it as a means of reassuring the staff that steps were being taken to ease the pressure of work. Management evidently envisaged that Operation Major *would* relieve some of the problem by "removing itinerant claims". The apparent reason for postponing the introduction of appointments for urgent cases was that the new system would "scare claimants off". Staff believe that the senior officers who planned the operation wanted to net as many claimants as possible: the claimants were virtually being set up.

On September 2 the manager, one assistant manager and two special investigators from the DHSS regional headquarters were at the South Oxford Middle School. The counters were staffed by officers from the unemployment benefit office – not from the DHSS. The next day, volunteers from Marston Road DHSS office were recruited to do the normal job of paying out benefits. It is said that one of the special investigators took over some counter work for a short time and didn't know how to deal with the forms. This may have been the source of a rumour that the office was being staffed by police on September 3.

DHSS endorsement of Cronin

The DHSS does not technically refer claimants to specific accommodation, but it hands out lists of suitable addresses, and claimants were still being directed from the DHSS to Cronin's and Patel's right up to, and immediately after, the arrests. Cronin's has now been promoted to the status of a "safe" address for the dispatch of giros. The DHSS has provided the landlord with a strong box in order for giros to be kept for residents. This is a new and puzzling distinction. One possible explanation for it could be that it may enable the DHSS to keep a closer watch on activities at 137 Iffley Road.

Summary

Pressures on staff

At a period of steeply rising caseloads, it is plainly inappropriate for the DHSS to cut staff levels in local offices. The Urgent Cases Regulations are useless unless an immediate decision is made on a

---

SUPPLEMENTARY BENEFIT

The Supplementary Benefit Act 1976 establishes a general right to benefit for "every person in Great Britain of or over the age of 16 whose resources are insufficient to meet his requirements" (section 1). A person's 'requirements' are set out in the Supplementary Benefit Regulations which establish different rates of benefit for people in different circumstances. In September 1982, single householders received supplementary benefit (SB) of £23.25 a week, plus an amount to cover their housing costs. A homeless person received SB of only £18.60 a week. This rate is paid on a day-to-day basis – in September 1982 it was £2.65 a day. A young homeless person, under 18, received even less – only £14.30 a week or £2.05 per day. All the rates were increased on November 22 1982; nevertheless the differentials between householders, the homeless and boarders remain equivalent.

Supplementary Benefit for boarders is calculated on a different basis. Boarders receive SB made up of three parts:–

a) the actual weekly charge of their hostel, lodgings or bed and breakfast;

b) an addition for meals not provided within that charge at a 1982 rate of 90p for breakfast and £1.25 each for lunch and evening meal; and

c) an amount for personal expenses. In September 1982 this was usually £7.70 a week for a single person.

Hence a person living in a hostel that provided no meals and who had to eat all meals in cafes received a meals addition of £23.80 plus £7.70, totalling £31.50 each week to spend on food, clothes, leisure and amenity items. This total reflected the cost of eating out more closely than did the homeless person's weekly SB of £18.60.

claim. It is clear from the delays experienced by all claimants waiting to have their cases assessed that the system is in chaos. The fact that at the time of going to press 12 local offices were on strike over staff levels proves that Oxford is not an isolated case. The frustration of officers was emphasised by the strong support for a one-day national DHSS strike on December 3 in protest at inadequate staffing levels.

Punishing claimants

Why did the DHSS pursue the claimants, when for years they have been aware of the dubious practices of profiteering landlords? Undoubtedly, a thorough investigation of the landlords would have consumed more DHSS staff time than the 'easy' option of a single swoop against claimants. It was possibly the relative simplicity of the scheme that prompted the local office to throw in its lot with the police – not to mention the 'savings' to be made in future by deterring the poor from making genuine claims. In justifying Special Claims Control, the Government has said that the innocent have nothing to be afraid of. Those arrested on September 2 know emphatically that the innocent do have reasons to fear.

No room for single homeless people in the city of 20,000 students.

THE HOUSING CRISIS 6

Single homeless in Oxford

There have always been a large number of single homeless people in Oxford – far more than, say, Swindon, a town of comparable size only about 20 miles away. Various reasons have been advanced for this: local employment opportunities in the fifties and late sixties which subsequently dried up; the existence of Oxford Prison and the Ley Clinic, both of which used to have particularly wide catchment areas. But the most important factor seems to be the city's acute shortage of private rented housing. The University has long refused to meet its own accommodation needs, and with 20,000 students overflowing into the private sector there is scarcely any place left for the single homeless. Since the onset of the recession, the situation has become very much worse: Oxford Cyrenians estimate that since 1976 the numbers of homeless people in Oxford have risen by some 400 per cent.

The report *Single and Homeless* (Department of the Environment, 1981) found that institutionalisation was an important factor in the process of homelessness: almost half of those interviewed in the survey had spent time in institutions. This may well be borne out among the middle-aged population of single homeless people in

Oxford. But a high proportion of Oxford's single homeless are young. In April 1982, a working party of the City's probation, health, housing and social services carried out a survey of young people up to the age of 25 who used the agencies which the working party represented. Interviews with 99 young people revealed that 47 were literally homeless (though only four said they were sleeping rough), with a further 20 threatened with imminent homelessness. Just over half the young people in the sample were between the ages of 18 and 20; just over a quarter were female and the majority (84) were white British (7 were black, 5 Irish and 2 Asian). Only six had jobs. The greatest proportion had left home because of a family dispute – family breakups and parental disputes being the most common reasons for young people to leave home identified by the researchers in *Single and Homeless.*

Lack of access to housing

Behind any assessment of housing provision in the city of Oxford are two incontrovertible facts. The first is that vacancies barely exist in private sector rented accommodation because of the large numbers of students, and because of the University practice of buying up housing in the city for lease as student accommodation. Scarcity pushes up rents: a room in poor accommodation can cost as much as £25 a week. The second is that even without the constraints of the recession, Oxford Council would probably not be able to build the housing it so desperately needs because there is very little land to build it on. The city's open spaces are privately owned by schools and colleges, while land outside the ring-road which skirts the city boundary is the province of the county council.

However, councillors admit that the local authority could, and should, have built more housing than it actually did. The Council has been building only 150-200 units a year in recent years, whereas 500-800 units ought to have been the target. There is now a possibility of acquiring two sites which will provide enough land for two years' building needs, and a programme is planned which is well in excess of the Government's current housing investment programme (HIP) allocation to the city. (For 1982/83 Oxford received only £4 million – about one third of what it bid for.) The shortfall will be made up from capital asset sales – including an airport, sold for £1.5 million – and, ironically, from the sale of council houses.

As elsewhere in the country, the demand for family housing in

Oxford is very great and singles have no priority. In response to the arrests, the Council has approached the Department of Environment for extra money to cope with single homelessness. But councillors are adamant that if money is not forthcoming, they cannot afford to divert funds from urgently needed family housing.

Who gets council housing?

The Housing (Homeless Persons) Act

The Housing (Homeless Persons) Act 1977 imposed a statutory duty on local councils to provide accommodation for households "in priority need" who become homeless. However, the groups identified by the Act as "priority" exclude single people except where they are vulnerable on the grounds of old age, mental illness or handicap, or some other special reason (such as the risk of violence to battered women without children if they return to their former home; or the risk to homeless young people of financial and sexual exploitation). The result has been that the overwhelming majority of those housed as a result of the Act have been families with children; only a tiny minority have been single people of working age.

Oxford City Council claims it is hard pressed to fulfil its statutory obligations to homeless families – let alone house single people. There were 34 homeless families in council-funded bed and breakfast accommodation in April 1982, and by the end of the quarter (in June) the number had fallen by five. Eighteen homeless households were given permanent accommodation over the period. They either came from b&b, or from "emergency rooms" in the homeless families hostel at Cowley Barracks – literally a disused barracks, now run by the Council and notorious for its damp, unsavoury, overcrowded conditions – or from some other form of interim accommodation. Only two of those rehoused (both from Cowley Barracks) were single people. Nine new families went into Cowley; seven direct into short-life interim housing; one direct into permanent accommodation as a licensee and six as tenants. A total of 19 single people approached the Council for housing under the Housing (Homeless Persons) Act during the same quarter. One was put into bed and breakfast. The rest were turned away.

Allocations from the waiting list

There are over 3,000 households on Oxford's housing waiting

list (7,000-8,000 people). Single people are only considered for housing from this list when they reach 55, an unusually stringent qualification which local groups have long been campaigning to change. However, there is a sub-section of the waiting list for single people under the age of 45. This list-within-a-list, some 450 strong, is not 'active' but is used by the Council to make referrals to housing associations. In rare cases – usually of severe health or social hardship – allocations are made to council property. For the quarter ending in June 1982, a total of 148 households were allocated council housing from the waiting list, of which seven allocations were to single people 'under 45'.

Where do single people go?

Against this background, the chance for single people to get decent permanent accommodation in Oxford is clearly remote. Over the last year, eight people have moved from the Cyrenians' Simon

Private housing at Friar's Wharf, Thames Street. These houses ought to have been council homes, but the valuable site was sold to a private developer by Oxford City Council's Conservative administration in the mid-seventies. The houses were completed in 1980. They look out over the river and sell for around £33,000, but three are still empty.

Martin Stott

House hostel into local authority accommodation. But this is a record – indeed, despite the Cyrenians' well-established links with local statutory agencies, it is more than in all the previous 13 years of Simon House's history, and is entirely the product of work by a new referral team.

Present provision for the single homeless is not only inadequate but is largely confined to the needs of special groups – those leaving psychiatric hospitals; the old, sick and long-term homeless; people on bail or probation; recovered alcoholics. It is significant that homelessness alone is not recognised as a need if you are single. The only people provided for are those whose homelessness is compounded by another 'problem'.

The Council had, for some time, been hoping to acquire a property for use as a night shelter but had failed to win sufficient support for the scheme. The arrests prompted a change of heart on the housing committee and the proposal has now been voted through. The shelter will provide 70 bed spaces in dormitory accommodation and will be run by the Salvation Army. This plan is nothing more than a stop-gap. Nor is it likely to find much of a place in the residents' affections. *For the building acquired by the Council is none other than the South Oxford Middle School – scene of the arrests.*

In addition to acquiring the school, a consortium has been set up between the Council and voluntary agencies to discuss leasing properties to groups for use as accommodation for the single homeless. But so far, no suitable properties have been found. The Council has also considered taking on private guest houses of the 137 Iffley Road type and running them for homeless people on the basis of "better the Council than the private landlord". However, council-run boarding houses would be an unsatisfactory solution because they would continue to prop up the ailing benefits system and divert funds from the provision of permanent housing.

What do single homeless people need?

The underlying need is for rented housing – local authority and housing association – in which single people can settle down permanently. This should cover a range of provision, including fully independent flats and reasonable individual bedsits, as well as more supportive provision for those with special needs.

Single people are no small minority of the population; they account for one in four of all households in England and Wales. It is officially predicted that the number of single people of working age needing independent housing will rise by more than half a million in the next decade.

The traditional assumption has been that single people could rent housing from private landlords, although in reality the accommodation was often insecure and unsatisfactory. The irreversible decline of the private rented sector now makes even this impossible for many. Yet local authorities still tend to concentrate their efforts on providing homes for families with children or the elderly. Few have recognised the scale of housing need amongst single people and re-shaped their housing policies accordingly.

The Government's policy is to encourage home ownership by every possible means. Yet even with a secure income this is more difficult for a single person to achieve than for a working couple; and few single people have gained the right to buy their council homes, since they haven't had council homes in the first place. In almost all areas of the country, finding somewhere decent to live is a nightmare for single people and these difficulties have been aggravated by the rise in unemployment, especially among the young.

Yet even if local authorities had the will to do more, the drastic cuts in government funds for housing investment would make this difficult. The number of new homes started by local authorities, new towns and housing associations has fallen from 168,447 in 1976 to only 36,725 in 1981, and the decline is to continue.

Between 1979 and 1984 the Government will have *halved* its total expenditure on public housing. It is ironic that at the same time it has allowed landlords to make fortunes out of public money by providing low-quality accommodation for the single homeless. Cronin's profits come from a system the homeless don't want and the tax-payer can ill afford. The money should be spent on providing decent, permanent homes for single people at reasonable rents.

Conclusions & Recommendations

Housing

1. Behind the violation of civil rights, the maladministration of justice, the biased media coverage, the profiteering by landlords and the inadequate system of social security benefits, lies one problem which was at the root of the whole operation: the lack of decent rented housing available to single people, especially claimants and others with very low incomes. With adequate housing, single homeless people would not be forced to choose between sleeping on the streets and making use of the accommodation offered by landlords such as Cronin and Patel.

Urgent action is needed to give single people access to satisfactory accommodation and to protect them from exploitation in the private sector. First, **the Housing (Homeless Persons) Act 1977 must be extended by a planned, agreed timetable to include all homeless people.** This demand was made to the Secretary of State for the Environment in July 1982 by an all-party deputation from the CHAR parliamentary committee. In a House of Lords debate in November 1982, successive speakers from the Labour, Conservative and Liberal benches, and the Bishop of Bath and Wells, called for the extension of the Act as an urgent Government priority.

A number of local authorities have recently endorsed policies for extending the range of homeless people who are accepted as being in priority need. At the very least, all local authorities must implement the existing legislation properly. This means they must not abuse the clauses relating to 'intentional homelessness' and must interpret the term 'vulnerable' in a flexible and sensitive way. Only if single people who are homeless have a legal right to accommodation will it be possible to insist on the elimination of totally unacceptable provision, such as the bed and breakfast establishments described in this report.

2. **The Rent Acts must be strengthened to protect all residential occupiers against arbitrary eviction and the erosion of their rights to minimum standards of repair, amenities, management and proper control of rent levels.** The House of Commons Select Committee on Environment, in its report on the Private Rented Sector, unanimously called for Government action to close the loopholes in the Rent Acts. The only effective means of achieving this is through a system of licensing by local authorities, which exempts genuine hotels and boarding houses for tourists and business users from control, and extends Rent Act protection to all other lettings.

3. Legislation is also needed to **control standards in houses in multiple occupation, particularly to enforce proper fire precautions and repairs.** Since 1978 there is documented evidence of 52 fire deaths in hostels and lodging houses – including the tragic fire in Clanricarde Gardens, London, in December 1981 when eight people died and 100 were made homeless. The existing laws are weak, cumbersome and largely discretionary. In February 1983 a Private Member's Bill will be introduced in Parliament to strengthen the law on houses in multiple occupation. All possible support is needed to persuade the Government to give its support to this issue.

4. **All local authorities must be urged to review their policies towards single people.** CHAR has recently published its *Blueprint: Local Housing Policies for Single People*, which spells out the kind of action needed. This must include a realistic assessment of demand; plans to provide a range of accommodation; removal of all barriers to access (such as rigid age barriers like the one operated by Oxford City Council); and action to remedy sub-standard conditions. The fundamental recognition must be that the great majority of single people want ordinary independent accommodation. Single homeless people should not be forced tc

tolerate night shelters or lodging houses which fail to offer the security, privacy and standards of basic comfort which every citizen should have a right to expect.

One immediate requirement is that Oxford City Council should review its policies towards single people in the light of the above recommendations. In particular, it should develop plans for a range of satisfactory housing. The establishment of an emergency night shelter in the South Oxford Middle School in no sense represents an adequate response to the housing crisis facing single homeless people in Oxford.

5. **The Government must enable local authorities to make a major expansion in their programmes of investment in good, rented housing.** Public expenditure on housing has been cut more drastically than any other area of social spending. In 1983/84 housing expenditure is less than one fifth of defence expenditure. Even after recently announced increases, spending on housing will be just under £3,000 million. Defence expenditure will be over £15,000 million. Although the reduction in housing expenditure has been continuous under both Labour and Conservative governments, the cuts over the last three years have been particularly severe. Between 1979 and 1984, the Government will have *halved* its total expenditure on public housing.

Benefits

6. A person of no fixed abode receives no assistance with housing costs, because there are none. Yet there is clearly a necessity to meet the costs of food, which is higher in the case of homeless people than for those who can cook meals for themselves. The homeless have to eat hot food in cafes. In this, their situation is identical to that of another category of supplementary benefit claimant – boarders whose lodgings or hostel do not provide meals. For boarders the standard payment (at 1981/82 rates) was £1.25 each for lunch and dinner, and 90p for breakfast. It would therefore seem logically inconsistent for the daily rate of benefit for a homeless claimant to be less than £3.40. This would give a weekly rate of £23.80 for food alone.

The weekly amount of benefit, however, does not only have to meet food. Regulation 4 of the Supplementary Benefit Requirements Regulations sets out what this amount of benefit is intended to cover, effectively stating that the money paid out should meet normal expenditure on day to day living, except for housing costs such as rent.

Homeless claimants will not have to meet household expenses, but they will still have to meet expenditure relating to clothing and footwear, travel costs, and leisure and amenity items – some of which may be greater than for people who have somewhere to live. It is therefore clear that **the supplementary benefit rate for single people without accommodation should be no less than the sum of a boarder's meals and personal expenses allowances.**

7. The only duty in relation to the time by which benefit offices should make decisions on a claim for benefit is contained in Regulation 2 of the Determination of Questions Regulations. This states that decisions should be made "so far as practicable... within 14 days". There is nothing in the Urgent Cases Regulations or elsewhere which requires a more immediate decision on an application made in urgent need. **There should be a duty stated in the Urgent Cases Regulations that an application for payment under those regulations should be decided forthwith.** This will have implications for the staffing and organisation of local offices (see below).

8. There is grave concern, both within the unions working in local offices and outside, that the staffing levels have been pared down too far. In addition, the concentration on fraud work seems to have had an adverse effect on the processing of routine claims. **There should be adequate staffing levels within local offices to ensure that claims are dealt with efficiently and quickly and in particular that applications for urgent needs be dealt with forthwith and other claims within the 14 day limit intended.** The DHSS should further enquire into the quality of service which local offices provide and take any necessary action to increase staff to adequate levels.

The Police

9. The police operation and the attempts to question it at the meetings of the Thames Valley Police Authority on September 24 and November 26 1982 show only too well how little democratic control there is over the police. **The Thames Valley Police Authority should mount a full and thorough investigation into the conduct of the Thames Valley Police during Operation Major.**

10. In order to ensure effective local control over the police, **legislation should be introduced to set up fully-accountable police authorities.** These would have powers to approve policing

policies and the appointment and dismissal of senior officers, as well as exercise control over resources, staffing and training.

11. In addition to this, **there needs to be an effective system for enforcing complaints against the police,** with a fully independent investigative element. This would ensure that those people arrested and held without charge and in conditions of great discomfort would be able to obtain satisfactory redress.

The Government has a chance to legislate on these matters in the Police and Criminal Evidence Bill, currently before Parliament. Detailed proposals for amendments have been prepared by the National Council for Civil Liberties.

The Courts

12. The type of special courts used to hear the cases arising from Operation Major have been criticised a number of times in the past. With great pressure on magistrates to hear cases at speed and operate a tariff system of penalties, it appears that many of the rights normally accorded to defendants were curtailed: there was a great reluctance to give defendants access to legal representation, release them on bail or remand them for social enquiry reports. Sentences in many cases can only be described as exemplary. **We recommend that the Lord Chancellor's Department mount a full and thorough investigation into the conduct of the courts and whether the tariff system was correctly applied.**

13. We also believe that special courts are a wholly unsatisfactory way of dealing with offences and **we recommend that the Lord Chancellor's Department also investigate the special court system.**

14. **A new public prosecutions system should be set up for England and Wales to remove the responsibility for prosecutions from the hands of the police.** This would elicit an objective assessment of the evidence and the desirability of a prosecution before a case comes to court.

The Media

15. The response of the national media to Operation Major is to be deplored for its distortion of the facts and the lack of balance in the way the police exercise and the circumstances surrounding it were reported. **The National Union of Journalists (NUJ) should consider the implications of this report for**

Article 3 (on accuracy and distortion) and Article 4 (on rectification and the right of reply) of the NUJ Code of Conduct. The Union should also consider amending Article 10, covering discrimination on the grounds of race, creed and sex to include discrimination on the grounds of social and economic status.

16. **In addition, the NUJ and the Association of Cinematograph, Television and Allied Technicians (ACTT) should issue guidelines on the reporting of social security stories similar to the guidelines which already exist in their respective codes of pratice on the reporting of race relations.** There should be a greater use of specialist journalists on stories of the Operation Major kind – reporters who, even if they don't cover the story themselves, can brief those who do to ask relevant questions and present the given facts in context.

17. The success of the PR exercise mounted by the Police in Operation Major proved a formidable impediment to those seeking to put the other side of the story. **Community groups and relevant agencies should take initiatives to try to establish contacts with the press and inform journalists of the issues at stake,** so that when reporters cover a story they bring some background knowledge to it – and know where to turn for more.

Appendix 1

Thames Valley Police
Statement of witness
Statement of **Jeremiah Cronin**
Occupation **Guest House Proprietor**
Address 137 Iffley Road, Oxford.
Dated the 10 day of September 1982

I am the owner of properties at 131, 133, 137 and 141, Iffley Road, Cowley, Oxford. These four houses are known collectively as The Nanford Guest House, 137, Iffley Road, Cowley, of which I am the proprietor. Within these premises I can accommodate approximately 75 persons. I supply bed and breakfast accommodation and my guests consist of unemployed itinerant persons, tourists and contract workers employed locally. The unemployed itinerant persons consist of those receiving accommdation by way of 'voucher' and those who pay cash.

Unemployed itinerant persons are usually referred to the Nanford Guest House by the Probation Service, Department of Health and Social Security or personal recommendation. If there is accommodation available a letter to that effect is given to the itinerant, either by myself or a member of my staff. There is no charge made in respect of this letter. If such a charge is made it is without my knowledge. The itinerant then takes the letter to the Department of Health and Social Security where they are issued with a voucher. The majority of these people return to The Nanford Guest House with their vouchers, but not all. These vouchers are issued by the Department of Health and Social Security for a specified period, usually a week, to cover the supply of bed and breakfast accommodation.

Upon returning to The Nanford Guest House, the itinerant hands over his voucher, either to myself, or member of my staff after signing it. Accommodation consisting of bed and breakfast is then made available to the itinerant. At the end of the specified period the voucher is returned by me to the Department of Health and Social Security and I receive payment at the rate of £6 per night. At the expiry of the voucher the itinerant if he wishes to continue his accommodation must pay cash, again at the rate of £6 per night. The majority of itinerants who receive accommodation by way of voucher do not continue to do so when they are required to pay cash. A number of itinerants do not take full advantage of the accommodation offered when it is supplied by way of voucher but it is always available and I am unaware of anyone ever having been turned away.

Itinerants who pay cash should, and normally are, issued with a receipt. Payments are made in advance. Payments are only made in respect of the nights itinerants are resident.

Although the doors to the Nanford Guest House are usually locked about half past midnight residents can gain admission by ringing the front door bell and I have never known anyone being unable to gain admission.

During the period I am able to say that (defendant's name) was not resident at The Nanford Guest House, 137, Iffley Road, Cowley, and had not made any payment in respect of accommodation.

Appendix 2

An analysis by David Piachaud using the Government's Family Expenditure Survey estimated how a single person is likely to spend supplementary benefit:–

Item	*Expenditure per week*
Food	£10.55
Fuel, light, power	3.75
Tobacco	2.20
Alcoholic drink	1.75
Newspapers, magazines etc	1.00
Transport	1.00
Toilet goods, soap, laundry etc	.85
Clothing and footwear	.70
Miscellaneous	1.45
TOTAL	£23.25

(*The Times*, May 27 1981. Figures increased for November 1981 uprating).

Broken down into actual items of expenditure it becomes clear how inadequate this minimum income is. If a claimant required new clothes or a new pair of shoes costing, say, £10, it is difficult to see where the money could come from without hardship.

The Claimants' Defence Committee discuss Operation Major.

The publishers

CHAR is the national campaign for single homeless people. Its aims are to focus public attention on the housing, health and other community service needs of homeless single people and to present positive policy solutions to central and local authorities.

The **Child Poverty Action Group** is a charity concerned with the poor, particularly families.

The **Claimants' Defence Committee**, set up as a result of Operation Major, defends the right of all claimants, whether in Oxford or elsewhere, to have enough to live on.

The **National Association of Probation Officers** is the professional association and trade union for all probation officers in England and Wales.

The **National Council for Civil Liberties** is an independent organisation which campaigns in Britain to defend and extend civil liberties, freedom of speech and expression and the rights of individuals and minorities to equal treatment under just laws.